The Essential
EXECUTOR'S
HANDBOOK

Everything Yc

The

EXECUTOR'S
HANDBOOK

A QUICK AND HANDY RESOURCE FOR DEALING WITH WILLS, TRUSTS, BENEFITS, AND PROBATE

DAVID G. HOFFMAN
Attorney at Law

THE ESSENTIAL EXECUTOR'S HANDBOOK
EDITED BY PATRICIA KOT
TYPESET BY KARA KUMPEL
Cover design by Jeff Piasky
Cover icons by Palsur/shutterstock
Printed in the U.S.A.

To order this title, please call toll-free 1-800-CAREER-1 (NJ and Canada: 201-848-0310) to order using VISA or MasterCard, or for further information on books from Career Press.

B CAREER
P R E S S

The Career Press, Inc.
12 Parish Drive
Wayne, NJ 07470
www.careerpress.com

Library of Congress Cataloging-in-Publication Data

CIP Data Available Upon Request.

For my smart, funny, loving,
and beautiful wife, Diane.

CONTENTS

INTRODUCTION

As with any book, people will read this one for any number of reasons. But if you are reading it because you have lost a loved one, you have my most sincere condolences. I have worked with the dying, the wake they leave behind, and their grieving families for 35 years. In every case, somebody steps up to put things in order—what is generally referred to as "settling the estate." If that someone is you, you are an exceptional individual. Most want no part of it (except for the money, of course) and are more than happy to leave the task to someone else. But, like anything you have never done before, you are probably anxious and overwhelmed. Those feelings are completely normal. It's your first day at school and you are rightly frightened. You needn't be.

Your job will carry many titles. You may be called the executor or the administrator or the trustee. Or you may be all of these. Whatever title you bear, your job is the same: to marshal and distribute.

The term *marshalling* refers to marshalling the assets of the decedent. That is to bring them together; to locate, account for, and organize every item the decedent owned; as well as to organize the debts. You will need to decide what to keep, what to sell, and what to abandon or send to the city dump. This can be a daunting task, but as my late father was fond of saying, "just do it piecemeal." In short, this aspect of your job cannot be rushed. Your approach needs to be systematic— one foot in front of the other. No skipping.

Distribution is usually what you would expect: distributing money to the beneficiaries of the estate. But it also entails paying the decedent's debts (also known as disbursements). And all the while you are marshalling and distributing, the assets are most likely generating more assets in the form of income such as interest, dividends, and capital gains. And income is going to require income tax returns, both federal and state and sometimes many states.

If you didn't feel overwhelmed before, you probably do now. Not to worry. The point of this book is simple. Don't go it alone. And I am not merely referring to "call a lawyer." The lawyer plays a big part in settling an estate, but you are going to need more than just a lawyer. Among others, you will most likely need an accountant, a realtor, a banker, a broker, an appraiser, an auctioneer, and a host of bureaucrats. If you don't have one already, may I also suggest a good bartender—cheaper than a therapist and usually a lot more interesting.

The team approach is important for another reason. Even if you have never settled an estate before, the law treats you as an expert. So, if you make any serious mistakes, you, and you alone, are solely liable for whatever damage you do. By using a team of professionals, any mistakes will most likely be made by them and not you. You are still liable, but you will have a right to bring a claim against the person who is actually responsible.

You are probably wondering how long all of this is going to take. Unfortunately, in most cases, that is hard to estimate. I have, on rare occasion, helped an executor settle an estate in only six months. In other cases, the settlement process has dragged on for six or seven years. Every estate is different, and some that appear complex are not while those that appear to be easy at the outset become bogged down in problems you never saw coming. A large estate is not necessarily a difficult one, and small estates can be the worst. Accordingly, any prediction as to how long it will take to settle a particular estate is about as reliable as a weather forecast; probably somewhere in the ballpark or right about 80% of the time.

What follows is a more detailed description of your responsibilities and the people who are going to help you. You are going to learn some law, but just enough to help you understand why you are hiring these people and evaluate their performance. As I have said, all of the liability ultimately falls on you. Selecting the right team is as important as the work that they will do for you. There are times when you will be scared to death, lose sleep, and ask yourself why you ever took on this insane task. Don't fret about it. Just do it piecemeal.

Chapter 1

Meet Your Estates

That's right. I said estates. The term, "settling an estate" is a misnomer. It is a colloquialism used to refer to the process of gathering up *all* of the decedent's assets, from every source, paying off creditors, and then passing out what's left to heirs and beneficiaries. However, how this is actually accomplished varies depending on which estate you are attempting to settle. There are four estates: the Probate Estate, the Contract Estate, the Knick-Knack Estate, and the Trust Estate.

Now, my goal is to show you how to let others settle these estates for you, but you need to understand the basics because, as executor, you bear the bulk of the legal liability. You need to keep an eye on these people as the work proceeds.

The Probate Estate

The Probate Estate consists of assets that the decedent owned in the decedent's name alone, without a joint owner, without a beneficiary, and without a living trust (more about living trusts later in this chapter). These assets are unique since, when you die, there is only one way to get at them and that is through the court proceeding known as probate.

To understand why probate is necessary, let's do a thought experiment. Let's say that you are the branch manager of a local bank. One day I walk in and tell you that both of my parents have died and I present you with their death certificates. I then proceed to tell you that I am their only child. Then I ask you to release all of their checking, savings, certificates of deposit (CDs), and the contents of their safe deposit box to me. What do you say?

    A. "Well of course, Mr. Hoffman! We will do that right now. And would you like that in small bills?"

    B. "Well of course, Mr. Hoffman! We will do that right away. However, I am afraid that I am going to have to see some ID."

    C. "Yeah, I wish I could help you but, if I did, I would lose my job."

The correct answer is C. All I have really done is prove to you that two people have died. I have not proven that I am their child. I have not proven that I am their only child. I have not even mentioned their debts, liens, or tax obligations. If you gave me their money, the bank would be open to legal action by my siblings, my parents' creditors, the IRS, and if I were an imposter, by the real me. The last time banks were that trusting was just before the recession; and you see how that turned out.

What I should have done was make an appointment with the probate court. The court would give me a piece of paper that says I have been appointed executor. Then, and only then, would I come to you, the branch manager, and present you with my executor certificate. That is because the law grants immunity to anyone who deals with me as an executor. So, if I present you with an executor certificate, take the money, and skip to Switzerland, it's not your problem.

In short, probate exists mainly to protect financial institutions. But it also gives the executor authority to be the decedent's replacement. An executor can, among other things, sign tax returns, make claims, file laws suits, open new accounts, and decide who, when, and how to pay people. This power is so respected that

I often get requests for a probate certificate even when the asset in question is not a probate asset. Annoying to be sure, but it makes the point.

The Contract Estate

The Contract Estate consists of assets that pass to someone as the result of a contract between a financial institution and one of their clients. The agreement is simply that the bank, broker, or insurance company will transfer the account or its proceeds to a preselected beneficiary at the time of the client's death.

For example, you open a checking account with your spouse. The account is classified by the bank as joint with right of survivorship. You die. The checking account automatically belongs to your spouse because your spouse survived you. That was the agreement you both made with the bank.

Or perhaps you take out a life insurance policy on yourself. In the life insurance contract, you select your spouse to be the beneficiary. You die. The insurance company pays the proceeds to your spouse. Why? Because that's what they agreed to do.

In neither example was the bank or insurance company acting out of the goodness of their collective hearts. They had a contractual obligation to turn over the asset to the surviving spouse. Failure to do so would lead to a lawsuit, investigation by the state, punitive action against the responsible employee, and so on and so on. The only thing that the spouse has to provide is a death certificate.

The Contract Estate does not require the assistance of the probate court. As I explained earlier, the probate court would only get involved if there was *not* an agreement to pay a joint owner or beneficiary. So what happens if the joint owner or beneficiary dies first? In such cases, the Contract Estate asset has to be reclassified as a Probate Estate asset since there is now no agreement as to who should get it. For this reason, financial institutions allow for contingent beneficiaries or multiple joint owners.

Other examples of Contract Estate assets include jointly owned real estate, jointly owned cars, annuities, 401(k)s, and individual retirement accounts (IRAs).

The Knick-Knack Estate

The Knick-Knack Estate is comprised of physical objects. Those objects can be valuable items such as jewelry, fine art, or coins. But, more often than not, it's just clutter, crap, and junk. But valuable or not, the law treats it all the same. The legal term is *tangible personal property.*

It's time for another thought experiment. Imagine that your last-surviving parent has just passed away. You go to their home and look around. If their home is like the home of most seniors, it is crammed with things. There are the usual items such as furniture, photographs, and light fixtures, but there are also books, paintings, pots, pans, china, silverware, reproduction art, and novelty birthday gifts from cash-challenged grandchildren. And then there is the pyramid of unopened mail that reaches from the dining room table halfway to the ceiling. And you haven't even gotten to the basement and attic yet. There you find stacks of boxes containing old clothes, old toys, old appliances, and even more unopened mail.

The bad news is that the Knick-Knack Estate is the most time-consuming and difficult estate to settle. The good news is that no court or financial institution is required. Technically, items of tangible personal property are classified as probate assets. However, the probate court only cares if your parents' wills specifically bequeathed their collection of Scottish curling stones to your impoverished brother living 2,000 miles away. (It's going to be your responsibility to get them to him and spring for the shipping.) The rest of the Knick-Knack Estate can be tackled by dividing it into three piles.

Likely, the smallest pile is the heirlooms—things that friends and family would like to have as a remembrance of the deceased. When my parents died, I suggested that my siblings work out what they wanted and simply take it with them after the funeral. It went amazingly well, with not a single punch thrown. My father tried this same approach when my grandmother died. He suggested the same thing but not just to family. He invited mourners at the funeral to come back to her house and select some remembrance of Nana. Dad forgot, however, that Nana lived through the depression and did not trust banks. Cash was stashed under every bed and in every drawer and closet. Guests were leaving with portraits of the presidents, Alexander Hamilton and Benjamin Franklin. Clearly, it is not a perfect solution for distributing heirlooms. I will suggest other approaches in a later chapter.

The second pile is comprised of items that can be auctioned. As you will see, you can hire an auctioneer to wander through the decedent's home and label those items experience has taught him are salable. As a rule, jewelry and coins are not auctioned but, again, we will come back to them.

By far and away, the biggest pile is just junk. Its destination is not your living room and not the auction block. It's going to the dump. Later, I will outline your options for getting rid of it; but, I have to warn you, it is a hard thing to watch your childhood bedroom set drive off to a landfill.

The Trust Estate

I am referring here to assets held by a living trust. A living trust is a document that states who is in charge of trust assets (i.e., the trustee), who is going to receive the benefit of those trust assets (i.e., the beneficiary), and who is creating the trust (i.e., the settler). The trust is then "funded" by, once again, securing the agreement of your financial institutions to hold your money in trust accounts.

What all of this means is that, when you die, your trustee has immediate access to those accounts for payment of debts and distributions to beneficiaries. Like the Contract Estate, the Trust Estate does not require probate. However, unlike the Contract Estate, the Trust Estate is capable of providing for multiple generations of contingent owners and beneficiaries.

For example, let's say that you are a widow with five grown children. All of those children have children of their own, and all of those grandchildren have children. Your living trust can be written in such a way that, should your children predecease you, their share is divided among their children—your grandchildren. If grandchildren predecease you, their share is divided among their children, your great-grandchildren; and so forth down the line of your descendants. If you have no descendants, the trust document looks to ancestors (e.g., parents, grandparents). But chances are good that they have already died. So it looks collaterally to brothers, sisters, nephews, nieces, and cousins first, second, and third removed. In short, with most trusts, we almost always know who the beneficiary is. As a result, the probate court gets the day off.

A living trust is also capable of retaining assets "in trust" for minors. There is nothing in the law that says that your children need to get their inheritance the moment you die. In fact, in most states, you simply cannot give money to persons under the age of 18 because they have no right to own it. Instead, most living trusts have a Minor's Clause that specifies the age that the child will ultimately get the money. Most of my clients pick 21, 25, or 30 years of age. One picked 60.

And that brings me to children with questionable money skills. It is possible to write a minor's clause that specifies no age of distribution. It simply says that the trustee will watch over your bitter disappointment for life, distributing only so much money as the trustee, from time to time, sees fit. In such arrangements, there is the added benefit that the child cannot lose the money to creditors or greedy spouses (because the child is also a sucker for a pretty face). And all of this flexibility is accomplished without probate.

Summing Up

It is possible that you will not have all four estates to settle. It is also possible that you will win a Noble Prize or win this week's Powerball. Sadly, these days, chances are good that you will probably be settling all four of the estates I have described; perhaps not in equal proportion but definitely something in each. Much like children, each has its own personality. And just like children, you will need the aid of different professionals to help them along their way. Some professionals assist in the settlement of all of the estates and some are unique to, say, only the Knick-Knack Estate. Your only job is to identify the estate to which an asset belongs, hire the correct professional to deal with it, and then go make yourself a drink.

Things to Do

1. Locate the original will.
2. Locate the trust (if there is one).
3. Order the death certificates (at least 10).
4. Locate the most recent statements for all bank and investment accounts. Note on each how they are held (joint, trust, or just decedent's name).
5. Photograph each room of the decedent's home(s) or other property (to identify items that may be removed in the future without your permission).
6. Locate all real estate deeds.
7. Locate all titles to vehicles.
8. Locate all life insurance policies.

Chapter 2
Meet Your Team

In Chapter 1, you learned about the four kinds of estates: the Probate Estate, the Contract Estate, the Knick-Knack Estate, and the Trust Estate. Now it is time to meet your team. They are (in no particular order): lawyer, accountant, appraiser, realtor, auctioneer, insurance agent, banker, broker, assorted bureaucrats, and the people who haul away a lifetime's worth of junk. Some of your team members will help you with all four estates, and some will take charge of only one. In later chapters, you will learn the job and responsibilities of each team member in detail. The purpose of this chapter, however, is to give you an overview—a chance to meet your team.

The Lawyer

The law is everywhere and effects almost every aspect of our lives. This is especially true in the case of settling estates. While lawyers may not be realtors, they know property law. While lawyers may not be accountants, they know tax law. And while lawyers may not be bankers, they know banking law—in particular, the Uniform Commercial Code. And so it goes with each member of the team. As such, one of the lawyer's principal responsibilities is to coordinate the efforts of the team as a whole and prevent one member from doing the job of another. For example, if the lawyer is going to prepare the Federal Estate Tax return (as many do), it is important that the accountant be aware of this so that it is not prepared twice.

In addition to coordinating the team, it is the lawyer who guides you through a court proceeding known as probate: gaining access to assets that were held in the decedent's name alone. And finally, the lawyer acts as negotiator, helping you deflect complaints from and among your decedent's beneficiaries as well as settle the claims of your decedent's creditors (usually at a substantial discount).

The Accountant

The accountant's principal job is as tax preparer. The accountant will be responsible for preparing the decedent's final tax return as well as preparing the annual tax returns of both the Probate and Trust estates. The accountant will also act as counsel. Questions such as whether it is a good idea to distribute income to beneficiaries or what is the tax effect of selling property are directed to your accountant.

The accountant also serves as liaison with the Internal Revenue Service. Should you forget to file a tax return or should you fail to pay the tax, the IRS will impose substantial penalties on the Probate and Trust estates. It is the accountant who will negotiate a reduction in these penalties. Many times, an experienced accountant can eliminate the penalties altogether.

The Appraiser

There are two kinds of appraisers: one for real estate and one for personal property (e.g., jewelry). The real estate appraiser is necessary for two reasons. First, you will need to know what your real estate is worth so that you will not waste time asking too much for it. On the flip side, you don't want to ask too little or you will become the target of vengeful beneficiaries. Furthermore, by providing a high value that the IRS will accept, the appraiser makes it possible to reduce capital gain tax when you sell the property.

The appraiser of personal property ensures that the knick-knacks are distributed fairly. For example, I know of a case where the executor divided two diamond rings between two sisters. The rings appeared to contain identical stones but, in reality, one stone was diamond while the other was cubic zirconium. The executor, in that case, opened himself to a lawsuit by the cubic zirconium sister.

The Realtor

For most people, real estate is the most valuable asset they will ever own. And so it follows that the decedent's real estate is the most valuable asset in your estates. Therefore, an excellent realtor is an absolute necessity. The realtor will take responsibility for putting the home on the market (i.e., listing), promoting the sale of the home (i.e., marketing), accepting or declining offers for you at your direction (i.e., contracting), and completing the sale of the home (i.e., closing).

Realtors are also expert in the daunting number of regulations that govern the sale of real estate these days. Your realtor will guide you through the maze of regulations, as it is critical that you comply with all of them. Failure to comply will result in some pretty stiff penalties. Not to put too fine a point on it, but executors who attempt to sell without a realtor may as well just stand in front of an oncoming train.

The Auctioneer

The auctioneer's job is to tell you which of the stuff lying around the decedent's home is worth something and can therefore be auctioned and which stuff lying about the decedent's home is just trash. In short, the auctioneer forces you to accept that things that may have sentimental value for some are, in fact, valueless to everyone else.

Having sifted the assets from the refuse, most auctioneers will then hold both in-person and online auctions. As a result, you receive the proceeds very quickly. The auctioneer's value then is in speed and efficiency. Your only alternative is a yard sale.

The Insurance Agent

With regard to the decedent's life insurance, your insurance agent will most likely be the decedent's insurance agent. While it is certainly possible to file a claim with the insurance company without the agent's assistance, why would you want to? Completing claim forms can be time-consuming, especially where there are multiple beneficiaries. The agent will usually do this for you at no charge. You have a million other things to keep track of. Take help when you can get it.

However, life insurance is not the only insurance that should concern you. You are also responsible for the safety of the estate assets themselves. Accordingly, it is imperative that you maintain or replace insurance on real estate, vehicles, and valuable personal property. If you like the decedent's agent, there is no reason to change horses, as it were. But if not, then you have a duty to find an agent you trust will provide the proper coverage.

The Banker

Probate Estates and Trust Estates need checking accounts just like you or me. A banker familiar with estate work will be able to set one up for you in no time at all. All that is needed is a death certificate and a Federal Identification Number (supplied by your accountant).

A lesser-known function of the banker in estate work is financing. Since death is an automatic default on the decedent's mortgage, a mortgage company can insist that the entire mortgage balance is due immediately. Your banker can be invaluable in securing a new mortgage, thereby allowing you the time to find a buyer for the property. Additionally, if you are short on liquid assets (e.g., cash), your banker may be able to provide a line of credit secured by estate assets.

The Broker

Whether you are an executor, a trustee, or both, your generic title is a fiduciary. And as a fiduciary, you have many duties. One of the most important of these is the duty to invest. While the estate settling process grinds along, you can't simply stuff assets in a mattress. Instead, you must depend on your broker to convert unproductive assets, such as cash, into secure investments.

Since many people use multiple brokered accounts, a good broker will also be able to consolidate a decedent's hodge-podge of investments into one account. In this way, you have less paper to deal with and your accountant will have far fewer statements to review come tax time.

The Bureaucrat

Although you don't get to choose your bureaucrats, for good or ill, they are part of the team. If you want to change title to the decedent's car, there will be someone at the Department of Motor Vehicles telling you how it is done. If you need the deed to the decedent's home, you will be talking to an employee at the county land records office. And if the decedent's estate is audited, you will be coming face to face with an IRS auditor.

That being said, you may find that bureaucrats are people too and many of them genuinely want to help you. In fact, depending on how you ask, you may even get them to bend the rules from time to time. So it is probably best to start brushing up on your people skills.

The Hauler

Your hauler's job is just that: to haul away furniture, broken appliances, broken china, and whatever else the decedent had been using to make do. Your hauler needs to be efficient and thorough—and most are. I once saw a two-man hauling team remove 60 years of useless stuff from a four-bedroom split-level home in just over three hours.

In my opinion, this is one of the most valuable members of your team. As long as you're not a hoarder, you will experience sheer delight at watching someone else haul out what is, literally, tons of worthless stuff from the decedent's home. And since it is impossible to sell a house with 30 years of *National Geographic* piled up in a corner, your hauler is not only valuable, he is indispensable.

Summing Up

And that is your team. You may not need all of them, but chances are very good that you will need most of them—especially if the decedent owned real estate. However, you should never just break open the phone book and pick your team at random. Instead, you should use a service similar to Angie's List or the Better Business Bureau to ensure that there have not been multiple complaints filed. That being said, you should realize that there will always be one or two complaints because there will always be people who are never satisfied. In short, you will need to exercise good judgment in picking your team. Remember who is ultimately responsible for absolutely everything. That's right. It's you.

Things to Do

1. Contact the licensing agencies for the professionals (e.g., lawyer, accountant, appraiser, and realtor) to get referrals for those members of your team.
2. Select a review and referral service such as Angie's List to get referrals for the other members of your team.

Chapter 3

You: The Fiduciary

A fiduciary is anyone who undertakes a legal duty to act for another. This may be done by court decree (e.g., an executor) or it may be done by agreement (e.g., a trust agreement) or it may be accomplished merely by your consent to a nomination under a document such as a Power of Attorney or a Living Will. The fiduciary may be a natural person (i.e., 46 chromosomes) or corporate (e.g., a bank). But regardless of how you became a fiduciary, you must understand that it is a duty that should never be taken lightly as it requires that your every action be done with extreme care. In fact, you will be held to one of the highest standards of care the law can demand—if not the highest. As a result, you are exposed to extreme liability. And, let's be perfectly clear about something else. It is no honor. It is work—lots and lots of work. You can feel proud later, when you have accomplished your task without screwing up.

As you may have gleaned from the previous paragraph, there are many types of fiduciaries. But for our purposes, there are just four: the Executor, the Trustee, the Agent under a Power of Attorney (also called an Attorney in Fact), and the Agent under a Living Will. You may be one or all of these, so it is important that you understand what is being asked of you in each case.

The Executor's Role

Your role as executor will depend on whether there is a living trust as part of your decedent's estate plan. (It is fairly common practice for estate planning attorneys to create a living trust as the main vehicle for managing and distributing the bulk of the decedent's assets.) We will first consider your role if there is a living trust and then proceed to your role where no trust exists.

If your decedent had a living trust as part of a larger estate plan then you are executor of a pour-over will. A pour-over will has one beneficiary: the living trust.

In short, the will is merely a device that sweeps up assets that have not made it into the living trust. You, therefore, are like a sheep dog. Your job is to round up the stray assets and get them where they need to go. But, remember, as we discussed earlier, an executor only has authority over probate assets. So don't go trying to wrangle things that don't belong to you.

Before you can proceed with your sheep-herding duties, however, you will first need the approval of the Probate Court. Just because the will names you as executor doesn't make it so. Until one of the court clerks takes you through the qualification process, you are not the executor at all. Until that time, you cannot even tell anyone that you are the executor. At best, you are only the executor apparent. But don't worry. If you are at least 18 years old and breathing, you will probably qualify as executor. And, as we shall see in a later chapter, your attorney will help you with the qualification process.

Once officially appointed executor, your first duty is to "marshal" the probate assets (i.e., your stray sheep). Once that is accomplished, you have the duty to keep those assets safe until they can be distributed to the trustee of the living trust. Now, according to the law of most states, safekeeping does not imply merely preventing the loss, destruction, or misuse of those assets. Rather, it implies all of that plus putting the assets to work. If, for example, your decedent had a large checking account that was earning no interest, you would move the money to a certificate of deposit or some other safe investment that was actually earning interest. On the other hand, you could also merely sign over the account to the trustee and be done with it.

In addition to marshalling and safekeeping, you will be required to sign an assortment of court documents. In most states, these are notice to heirs and beneficiaries, the inventory, and one or more accounts (or accountings). You may also be required to sign the decedent's final tax returns, the Probate Estate's tax returns, state death tax returns, and possibly, even the Federal Estate Tax Return.

When you are executor of a pour-over will, that is about the extent of your duties. However, if there is not a living trust and the will itself specifies who gets the probate assets, you are going to be responsible for tasks such as paying bills, negotiating debts, selling real estate, and distributing whatever is left to the beneficiaries in a way that makes them happy so they don't sue you. You may also have all of these duties if there is no will at all and the court qualifies you as the administrator, because the administrator of a Probate Estate has the exact same job as an executor but without the impressive title.

The Trustee's Role

If your decedent has a living trust, your duties are similar to an executor when there is no living trust. That is, you will have duties such as safekeeping assets, paying bills, negotiating debts, selling real estate, making distributions to the beneficiaries, as well as signing tax returns. What you do not have is an obligation to answer to a court. Accordingly, unlike the executor, you will not be signing any court documents. But, let's look more closely at these duties.

Safekeeping: While the executor only has a duty to keep safe the probate assets, you, as trustee, must watch over all of the assets held in trust name when the decedent died as well as all of the other assets that may be coming your way. For example, the executor will be transferring all of the probate assets to you. Furthermore, the living trust may be the beneficiary of a number of assets from the Contract Estate, such as life insurance and retirement accounts. It is one thing to move some cash to a certificate of deposit. It is quite something else to file claims on a dozen or more small insurance policies and then, when the checks arrive, to put that money to work as well. And, as you will see in a later chapter, filing a claim on a retirement account has serious tax consequences and must be done carefully.

Paying Bills: If your decedent had creditors, they will probably be looking to the executor for payment. But when the estate plan consists of a living trust and a pour-over will, those creditors will probably be setting themselves up for disappointment since the executor will only have the stray probate assets. You, as trustee, will more likely have the ability to pay them. And while it can be entertaining to watch a creditor twist in the wind for a while, trying to determine who to harass, you should nevertheless take the high road and contact whoever makes a claim against the Probate Estate. If the bill appears to be legitimate, it should be paid.

Having said that, neither a trustee nor an executor has a duty to pay a debt that is not enforceable. So, for example, if a creditor is seeking payment for a credit card debt that was incurred a dozen years ago, chances are good that the enforcement of that debt is barred by your state's statute of limitations. Anytime you are unsure about your obligation to pay, check with your lawyer first.

Negotiating Debts

When a customer dies, most companies will first ask for payment of any debt the decedent owed (e.g., credit cards or service plans). If their request goes unanswered, they will usually employ the assistance of a debt collection company. The debt collector gets a commission for every dollar collected and is usually authorized to take less than the full amount in satisfaction of the debt. That gives you a degree of bargaining power. You may be able to satisfy the debt for as little as half of what is owed. However, not everyone is comfortable with trying to wiggle out of an obligation. Since it will be your lawyer doing the negotiating, you should make your feelings known.

Selling Real Estate

Trustees rarely sell securities without a very good reason. What they routinely sell is real estate. And, while that seems simple enough, you must always be conscious that some or all of the trust beneficiaries may not agree with your plans. They may disagree with the timing of the sale (e.g., sooner rather than later), the terms of the sale, the sale price in particular, or whether the property should be sold at all. You are going to have to broker an agreement among them before the mansion even goes on the market. If it later appears that you are going to have to deviate from that plan, you will need to get their unanimous approval for the change. Understand, of course, that you have the legal right to do what you think is best but it is tough to do your trustee job if you are always being addressed as "the defendant."

Making Distributions to the Beneficiaries

If there is the legal equivalent of a mine field, this would be it. One never knows when a beneficiary is going to howl about who got what, when, and why. We will explore this problem in more detail in a later chapter. However, as a rule of thumb, make no distributions without first consulting your lawyer.

Signing Tax Returns

In a nutshell, you are responsible for what you sign. Even though your accountant and your lawyer will be preparing the tax returns, you will be the one audited. An argument that you were not the preparer will hold about as much weight with the IRS as a soaked tissue (single ply). Accordingly, review every return before you sign it.

The Agent's Role Under a Power of Attorney

First things first. If you are settling a decedent's estate, any power of attorney the decedent had signed in life is now defunct. All powers of attorney die with the person who made them. However, yours may be a case where no one has yet died, though death may be imminent. In such a case, you can use the power of attorney given to you by a "principal" to move assets into your principal's living trust. You do this by deeding real estate into the trust name and re-naming bank and brokered accounts to the trust name. You can also use the power of attorney to change life insurance beneficiaries to the trust name and possibly change retirement account beneficiaries to the trust name, especially where the trust beneficiaries are minors and couldn't legally accept anything paid to them directly.

What's more, as in many cases, your principal has been disabled for many years. Laws have changed and you need to amend the trust to conform to the new law. You can use your power as agent to do that as well. Just two years ago, in Virginia, the legislature renumbered a large swath of the Virginia Code (i.e., Virginia's statutes). Clients who were still alive but had become disabled conformed their trusts to this change by having their agents sign the conforming trust amendments.

Yes, a power of attorney would seem like a wonderful thing. Something to spruce up a trust in the eleventh hour. Unfortunately, I am not aware of any law in any state that requires any person or institution to accept your power of attorney. You will likely be told that the power of attorney is too old, not specific enough, or simply that the institution doesn't recognize any power of attorney form but their own. It can be maddening. For this reason, your assistance as an agent under a power of attorney may be limited. Nevertheless, you have an important role in preparing the way for the executor or trustee. You may indeed have difficulty using your power to move assets into your principal's trust, but there should be no problem with signing conforming trust amendments. Your request for moving assets into a trust may be rejected, but the financial institutions will at least explain the problem as they see it. Without the power of attorney, it's extremely unlikely that they would even talk to you.

The Agent's Role Under a Living Will

Living wills go by many names. Depending on your state, they may be officially known as Health Care Proxies, Powers of Attorney for Health Care, or Advance Medical directives. And they have evolved from simple, "just pull the plug" documents to a litany of instructions ranging from life support specifics to burial directions. Regardless of the name or complexity of the document, the agent's role is to carry out these instructions. In the absence of a living will, the law looks to family to make the hard decisions. In other words, neither the executor nor the trustee has any say in the matter and so you cannot expect guidance from those quarters. But let's begin by looking at the most common instructions that you will be asked to carry out.

Removing Life Support

In the vast majority of states, removing life support means just that. There is a device or devices that are keeping a person alive. This could be a respirator or cardiac defibrillator. It could be intravenous hydration or feeding tubes. Or it could be all of these things. If the living will instructs you to remove life support, it is directing you to request that the hospital remove these devices. But there are a number of factors to consider.

First and foremost, does the patient's condition justify removing life support? In most states, the governing statute provides one or more threshold requirements. For example, in some states, the patient's death must be imminent and there is nothing that can be done to change the prognosis. In other states, in addition to "imminent death," the law may allow the removal of life support if the patient is in a "permanent coma" or a "persistent vegetative state." Further, it is important to understand that the removal of life support is not the same as euthanasia. In the case of the former, you are simply removing the technology that is keeping the patient alive. In the case of the latter, you are taking an active part in ending life. The first is widely accepted; the latter is not. That being said, you should know that very few states do permit euthanasia. You will need to check with your lawyer regarding the laws of your state.

Medical Treatments

It is no secret that doctors and hospitals are risk adverse. That is, they wish to avoid any actions that may result in a lawsuit. As the agent under the living will, you help them achieve a level of security. Imagine a family that cannot even begin to agree on their loved one's treatment. Who does the attending physician listen to? Who is in charge? Most states provide that, in the absence of a living will, there is a hierarchy of relatives who are in charge, usually beginning with the spouse and working on down from there. However, that is not always a reliable alternative. The physician and hospital will be looking to you, the agent named in the living will, to make the difficult decisions.

Organ Donation

Most people wish to donate their organs if that would help someone else. But be careful here. Who pays for the procedure of harvesting a heart or a kidney? If the document is silent on this point, you can assume that the cost will fall on either the Probate or Trust Estate. It is also important that you know whether organ donation includes whole body donation. Most living wills specify what is intended, but the patient may have written the living will himself or copied it from one of the many misleading, dangerous, and altogether useless documents available online. As a rule of interpretation, organ donation means taking an organ. Whole body donation usually means donating the decedent's remains to a medical school. However, it can also mean donating the decedent's remains to one of the many criminal forensic projects created to study human decomposition. These studies establish a database that can aid law enforcement in establishing a time of death in cases of murder or accident.

Disposition of the Remains

If your decedent had a preference for a particular disposition, the living will should provide that. The two most common dispositions, of course, are burial and cremation. However, the decedent may have had something more unusual in mind. For example, it is possible to have your remains prepared for freezing and then submerged in liquid nitrogen. The hope is that, when a cure is found for whatever killed you, your body can be thawed, repaired, and sent on its merry way. (Vegas is not giving very good odds on the success of such a procedure.) Or perhaps your decedent wished to have some or all of his ashes launched into space. There is, or at least there was, a company that offered such a service.

Regardless of the method of disposition, however, remember that it must comply with all federal, state, and local laws. For example, burial is legal but burial in your backyard is usually not. Cremation is legal but, unless you own a licensed crematorium, doing it yourself is probably not. And as far as the scattering of ashes is concerned, that is almost never legal and is usually done under the cover of darkness. A client once asked me to rewrite his living will to specify that his remains be dropped on the home of his lifelong enemy. When I told him that scattering ashes from an airplane was illegal, he replied, "Who's talking about ashes?"

Of course, it should go without saying that the role as the agent under a living will does not even begin until it has been determined that the patient cannot speak for herself. I once got a call from a client's very angry daughter. She said, "You know that living will you prepared for my mother? Well it doesn't work!" Feeling like I had suddenly walked into the middle of a Greek tragedy, I asked, "What has happened?" The daughter replied, "Mom is in the hospital and I demanded that she be removed from life support. But then the doctor asked Mom if that is what she wanted, and Mom said no. So they wouldn't do it!" The lesson here should be obvious. Be careful who you pick as your agent.

Multiple Fiduciaries

Most, if not all, states allow for co-fiduciaries. That is to say, you can have two or more acting executors, trustees, or agents. It is even rumored that George Washington's will nominated seven co-executors. There are advantages and disadvantages to such an arrangement depending on the type of fiduciary.

When an executor is from out of state (i.e., not the decedent's state of residence), the Probate Court will usually require that the executor be bonded. And bonds can get expensive. However, if the executor is paired with another who is a resident of the decedent's state, the bond can be waived. Unfortunately, co-executors usually must act in unison. After a few months of trying to agree on everything and to sign everything together, the bond may start to look like a bargain.

Trustees do not face a bonding problem, but there is still the problem of too many cooks and the ill-fated soup. The general rule is that there should never be more than one acting trustee. Anything else tends to slow the estate settling process. The same can be said of agents acting under a power of attorney or a living will.

The Appearance of Conflict

Whenever I give a lecture, I invariably get the following question: "If the will says that the estate is to go to Sally but the living trust says that the estate is to go to Sue, which one is controlling?" And, by now, you probably know the answer as well as I. There is no conflict because the will governs only the Probate Estate and the living trust controls only the Trust Estate. In fact, in the case of a pour-over will, the Probate Estate eventually becomes the Trust Estate.

The bigger problem, as I see it, is determining whether the decedent had intended for the will and trust to have different beneficiaries. If, for example, the decedent had written the will giving his fortune to Sally but later drafted the trust naming Sue as the lucky beneficiary, intending to disinherit Sally, there is no conflict over control but there is definitely an unintended result. That is, the Probate Estate will go to Sally even though that was not the ultimate desire. To avoid these sorts of problems, estate planning attorneys always draft a compatible will whenever they draft a living trust.

Summing Up

In the business of settling a decedent's estate, four different fiduciaries may play a role: the executor, the trustee, the agent under a power of attorney, and the agent under a living will. Each has their own distinct duties and obligations. Any conflict that arises does so among multiple fiduciaries of the same type. The apparent conflict between fiduciaries of different types (e.g., executor and trustee) is usually an illusion grounded in the belief that there is only one estate. These duties and obligations carry massive liability and should never be taken lightly. Consult your lawyer anytime your course appears to be getting murky.

Things to Do

1. Review the will and trust to see what role(s) you have been assigned.
2. Select a co-executor if you are not a resident of the decedent's state.

Chapter 4

The Lawyer: Courts, Contracts, and Crisis

Introduction

Everyone must deal with the law. That is especially true for people in business. The accountant is schooled in tax law, the realtor is schooled in contract law, and bankers and brokers swim in a sea of legal regulations. But while law governs the business of accountants, realtors, bankers, and brokers, for lawyers, the law *is* their business. Regardless of specialty, the lawyer is schooled in every field of law. As a result, one of the most important roles for the lawyer in settling an estate is to coordinate the rest of the team. Without a coordinated effort, the executor's job becomes chaotic.

For example, a contractor cannot begin repairs on a home until the auctioneer and the junk man have completely emptied the home. The realtor cannot list the home for sale until the contractor has made it attractive and livable once more. And the accountant cannot calculate the capital gain or loss until the property has been sold. Watching over all of this activity is the lawyer, as if conducting a symphony. But then, of course, there are jobs that are purely legal in nature and those are the topics of this chapter. Before we begin, however, it would be best to start with some legal definitions.

Terminology

Probate asset—any asset that the decedent died owning in his or her name alone and without a beneficiary.

Executor—a court-appointed individual who manages the probate assets.

Administrator—same job as executor when there is no will.

Will—a legal document that selects an executor and instructs the executor on how and to whom the probate assets are to be distributed.

Heirs at law—individuals who are entitled to the probate assets if there is no will.

Probate (or probate administration)—A court proceeding designed to help the executor get control of the probate assets and then oversee his actions.

Surety—the guarantee of a bondsman that, should the executor abscond with the probate assets, the bondsman will restore the value of the stolen assets.

Living trust—an agreement between a settlor and one or more financial institutions that provides that neither conservatorship nor probate will be necessary after the settlor becomes disabled or dies.

Settlor—one who establishes a living trust.

Trustee—one who manages the assets held in a living trust.

Conservatorship—a court proceeding, similar to probate, designed to help a conservator get control of a disabled person's assets and then oversee the conservator's actions.

Now that you have a basic understanding of the terminology, let us proceed to your selection of a lawyer. A more detailed Glossary is included at the end of this book.

Finding a Lawyer

Although lawyers are schooled in all areas of the law, the law has become so complex that the attorney who does it all has all but gone extinct. For professional, practical, and liability reasons, almost all lawyers now limit their practices to just a few fields of law. To settle an estate, you want a lawyer who specializes in probate, estate planning, and death taxation. It would also be nice if the lawyer has a background in accounting.

The usual way to find a lawyer is by referral. Referrals from your accountant, banker, or broker are preferable to referrals from family or friends unless your family or friends are accountants, bankers, or brokers. The problem with people who don't work with lawyers on a regular basis is that they don't appreciate the infinite permutations of legal cases. No two are alike. So advice like, "Yeah, my Aunt Beatrice died last year and her family lawyer took care of it. No problem," is, in fact, useless. For all you know, Aunt Beatrice may well have died destitute so there was nothing to settle while her family lawyer hasn't been in active practice for 20 years. If all else fails, you can always get a referral from the State Bar Referral Service. Every state has a bar organization that every lawyer in that state must join. The state bar knows what they do and how long they've been doing it.

First Meeting

Most attorneys have four goals for the first meeting: (1) gather information about the decedent, (2) gather information about the decedent's assets, (3) gather information about the beneficiaries named in the will and trust as well as information about the heirs at law, and (4) gather information on you, the executor/trustee. So, you will need to come prepared.

First, be sure that you bring at least two original death certificates as well as the original will and any codicils (i.e., amendments) to the will. The death certificate will give the lawyer most of the information he or she needs regarding the decedent. The will allows the lawyer to see if there are any obvious problems such as a will that is improperly signed, fails to name an executor, or is not properly witnessed or notarized.

You should also bring an informal financial statement that lists all of the decedent's assets, including bank accounts, retirement accounts, life insurance, real estate, investment accounts, debt information (i.e., mortgages, credit cards), and vehicles. The financial statement should also indicate how the asset was held: decedent's name alone, joint with another individual, or in trust. If the asset names a beneficiary (e.g., life insurance or retirement account), you need to know the name and address of the beneficiary as well as any relationship to the decedent. As for knick-knack assets, you probably only need to provide those items that the decedent had specifically insured (i.e., an engagement ring). If you are unsure how to do any of this, you can gather up the decedent's most recent statements (e.g., bank statements, broker statements, real estate tax bills) and bring them to the lawyer instead.

You will also need to provide the name, address, and relationship of each beneficiary named in the will (if there is a will) and in the trust (if there is a trust). If the decedent had neither a will nor a trust, you will need to provide this information about the decedent's spouse or children. In the absence of a spouse or children, the lawyer will walk you through the potential list of relatives who stand to inherit. And it is a long list.

Of course, if you are the executor, administrator, or the trustee, you will need to provide information on yourself. Most lawyers will take your word without checking your driver's license, passport, or birth certificate. If you don't provide the lawyer with accurate information, you will only be creating problems for yourself.

Many times at the first meeting, the lawyer will also suggest professionals who can make up the rest of your team. Lawyers are prohibited from taking money for such referrals, and most professionals are prohibited from paying for them. So you can be confident that, in most cases, the individuals or companies that the lawyer recommends are actually talented, experienced, and honest, and that the lawyer has worked with all of them in the past. And having a team that has worked together in the past will greatly expedite the whole process.

Finally, many attorneys will then schedule your probate appointment. On the date of your probate appointment, your lawyer will accompany you to the probate court where you will be sworn in as executor or administrator.

Probate

Not to put too fine a point on it but probate exists for only one reason and that is to protect financial institutions. As I mentioned in Chapter 1, financial institutions such as banks or brokerages face a potential swarm of litigation if they simply give you the decedent's money. However, the law provides that if the county or city court "qualifies" you as executor, the financial institution is absolved of all liability regardless of your nefarious plans or deeds. It then becomes the court's responsibility to keep an eye on you. How closely they watch you depends largely on demographics. If the county or city has a large, wealthy population, you are going to have to account for every penny that crosses your palm and account for those pennies in a timely fashion (i.e., deadlines). Failure to account or to do so in a timely fashion could result in jail time. On the other hand, if you reduce the population or make them poorer, the process becomes incrementally less formal. For example, I once had a case in a rural county of West Virginia. After they qualified my client as executor, we never heard from the court again.

But let us assume that the decedent died as a resident of a populous, wealthy county and that nobody is going to go easy on you. We will call it Difficult County. In that case, the probate process follows very clear steps and tolerance is at an absolute minimum. The terminology I use here was created for Virginia but, regardless of what they are called in your state, the steps are the same.

As you may have surmised, the first step in the probate process is called Qualification. You and your lawyer appear before a court clerk and you are asked for the death certificate. Then you will be asked for the original will and any original codicils (i.e., amendments to the will). Then the questions begin. Who are the decedent's heirs-at-law? What is the combined value of the probate assets? In some states, the clerk will ask you for both the combined value of the real estate as well as the combined value of the rest of the probate assets. Are the real estate values based on assessment or appraisal? Your lawyer will field all of these questions for you because, in most states, the clerk is not permitted to help you. For example, if you don't know what an heir-at-law is, the clerk will probably tell you to retain a lawyer and come back. The clerk is not just being difficult. Rather, to answer your question puts the clerk's job in jeopardy. Why? Because the clerk is not a lawyer and explaining a simple term for you is considered rendering legal advice and, thus, practicing law without a license. Crazy, huh? I guarantee you that the clerk of that small West Virginia county would have answered your question and not given it a second thought. But we are in a Difficult County here.

Let me give you an idea of how bad it can get in Difficult County. Many years ago, a man came to see me whose parents had died in very quick succession. The father had a will, but it contained a very problematic provision. It said that the estate was to pass to his wife *unless* she failed to survive him by 30 days. The wife's survived her husband by 31 days. I realized that we would have to go through the entire probate process for the father's estate to pass the probate assets to the dead wife. Then we would have to probate her estate in order to pass those same assets to the children. Since the father had all of the assets and his wife had none, the two estates were identical. I believed that probating the exact same estate twice would be an absurd exercise. So I went to see the fellow who oversaw all probate operations for that county. I told him that I had a case that, according to a strict reading of the law, was going to require the client to pay twice for the exact same work and that it would be an inefficient use of both his people's time as well as my people's time. I proposed that we simply combine the two cases and leave it at that. He pondered this for a moment and then said to me, "David that makes a lot of sense. But, no. I have never been sued. I am never going to be sued. In this county, we do things by the book." The matter took seven years to complete. In that time, the man who came to see me died. He had been the executor, so a new executor had to be qualified. Also, the youngest child called our office every day asking simply, "Where's my money?" I suggested he speak to the county official who had, thus far, never been sued.

After your lawyer has gotten you through the qualification process, you are sworn in as the executor. If there was no will, you will be sworn in as the administrator; same job, different title. The clerk will then give you certificates that proclaim you are the executor or administrator. You will provide these certificates to each and every financial intuition that requests them. In theory, only institutions holding probate assets need them, but I have been asked for the certificate by institutions that most certainly do not require them, such as a bank holding a trust account. Accordingly, your lawyer will probably advise you to get more certificates than it would appear that you actually need. But then your lawyer has learned that, for your average bank, broker, or insurance company employees, the law is simply what their manager tells them it is. Any attempt at explaining otherwise will fall on deaf ears.

The next step is to get an Employer Identification Number (or EIN) from the Internal Revenue Service. This number replaces the decedent's Social Security Number and is provided to all financial institutions holding probate assets. In years past, it took six months for the IRS to issue an EIN. Now it takes less than five minutes online. Either the lawyer or the accountant will obtain the number for you. If they have worked together before, each will know whose task that is.

Your executor certificate and EIN in hand, you then proceed to open a checking account for the probate estate. As a rule, a bank will not simply convert the decedent's checking into probate checking. A new account must be opened and the old account closed.

In Difficult County, you will have a short time to notify all of the beneficiaries of the will and all of the heirs-at-law that you have been sworn in as executor and that the probate case has begun. Typically, you have 30 to 60 days. Your lawyer will prepare and mail these formal notices. A few months after that you will have to provide the court with an inventory that describes all of the probate assets in detail and provides their respective values. Your lawyer will be preparing this for you as well.

Each year or two thereafter (depending on your state), Difficult County will expect to see a formal accounting of your progress. Your lawyer will prepare the accounts for you, which is why I recommend your lawyer have an accounting background. The account format is not "accounting" in the professional use of the word, but it is close enough to make an accounting background useful. When the last account is filed and you have demonstrated to the court that all of the probate assets have been properly disbursed and distributed, the probate process ends. In most cases, however, your job is not yet done. If there was a living trust, for example, you as executor have transferred the probate assets to you as trustee and your work continues.

While your lawyer will help you with a myriad of minor problems that arise, there are two legal functions that deserve special mention here. Your lawyer will help reduce the decedent's debts as well as mitigate family disputes.

Let us begin with a discussion of creditors. In every state, creditors have a hierarchy. The top dogs are those lenders who hold pledged security (i.e., mortgage companies) and lien holders (i.e., the IRS). At the bottom of the heap are the general creditors who own nothing more than the decedent's long-ago promise to pay them back. It is rare that your lawyer can reduce the amount owed on a mortgage. It is only slightly less difficult to negotiate the amount of a lien. On the other hand, general creditors accept their lowly standing as a cost of doing business. They are well aware that, after the mortgages and liens are paid, there may be nothing left for them. The lawyer will wait until the general creditor files its claim with the estate and then call them to discuss a settlement. Some lawyers wait for the creditor to use a collection agency knowing that the debt collector is working many, many cases and they are willing to reduce the amount owed in exchange for immediate payment. It is not uncommon for a collection agency to accept as little as 50% to settle the claim.

The question of morality is relevant here. Many executors believe that, if the decedent owed a debt, then it is only right that the debt be paid in full. I not only respect that point of view, I actually agree with it. But I am simply the lawyer. My job does not involve dispensing my opinion as to what is moral—only what is legal. The lawyer's job is to tell you your options and then do whatever you decide. This is one area where you are on your own.

And speaking of being on your own, never is that as true as in your dealings with your family. In particular, siblings are a huge source of stress and conflict. If you were selected to be the executor, it is most likely because you are viewed as the hard-working, responsible one. However, allowing you to do all the work does not mean that your siblings actually trust you— or each other for that matter. After you have said your goodbyes to your mother or father, brace yourself. You may be in for one or more storms headed your way.

The first possible tempest involves the decedent's personal effects. Siblings will often lay claim to their parent's personal effects with comments such as, "Dad promised me his Rolex," or "Mom promised me all of her jewelry," or "As we all know, I was told that I was to get all of the cash in the safe." I know of one case where an enterprising young man produced a handwritten note that listed each and every item he was promised. The note was not dated and signed simply, "DAD." Curiously, the note was not in the father's handwriting. The son explained that his father had dictated the note to him. Needless to say, your job, as executor, is to ignore all of it. If something was promised then it should have been in the will. If not in the will, then it should at least appear on a typed list indicating who gets what and bearing the signatures of all of the children. And to prevent the unauthorized removal of any personal property, you have a duty to secure the residence. This is not just a precaution regarding siblings but just about anyone who wishes to take what you have been given to protect. Call a locksmith and change the locks. Put monitored alarms on every door and window. Technically, all of the personal effects now belong to you and will remain in your care until a reasonable method of distribution can be determined.

Probably the best way of distributing the personal effects is to ask the siblings what they want. Sometimes, there is no conflict. Your lawyer would prepare what is known as a Beneficiaries Agreement, which describes the distribution of the items. You and your siblings then sign and notarize the agreement. Problem solved. But what if there is a conflict? Then it is up to you to decide. And your siblings need to be made aware of that. Your lawyer would address a letter to each of them on your behalf explaining that you have the right to appraise and sell all of the personal effects and that any item determined to be financially valueless, regardless of its sentimental value (e.g., photographs), will be hauled off to the dump. This may cool the conflict.

Another storm brewing on the horizon involves the make-up of each share. One child may want the home while another may want the investments. Provided you distribute shares of proper value, regardless of what comprises each share, you have done your job. But again, in the interest of family peace, it is best to ask what each sibling wants and then use a Beneficiaries Agreement to seal the deal. In settling my parents' estates, there were multiple agreements. But again, what if it is not possible to distribute the shares the way your siblings desire? Say, for example, your brother wants the house but he is only entitled to a third of the estate. If the house comprises half of the estate and your brother cannot finance the difference, you cannot do as he asks. If you are faced with an impasse, you can sell all of the estate—real estate, investments, personal effects, and so on—and just write checks. In all but the rarest cases, you have that right. Making your siblings aware of this may help negotiations.

Summing Up

These are only the most common tasks that your lawyer will undertake for you. There are far less common problems that your lawyer will tackle for you as well— everything from defending against a will contest to reviewing mineral rights contracts. Every case is different in some way. And, unfortunately, some cases are so different that they become nightmares unlike anything you could have imagined. But your lawyer has your back because your lawyer represents only you—not the estate and most certainly not the beneficiaries. So, when your job makes it seem like you're living in the Wild West with bullets and arrows whizzing by your ears, just think of your lawyer as a hired gun. Never hesitate to call when trouble is a-brewing.

Things to Do

1. Interview and select your attorney.
2. Provide your attorney with the original will and at least two original death certificates, as well as copies of each of the following: trust, recent bank and investment account statements, real estate deeds, vehicle titles, and life insurance policies.
3. Have your attorney schedule a time to qualify you as the executor.
4. Promptly provide anything else your attorney requires.

Chapter 5

The Accountant: Taxes Aren't Just for the Living

Decedents' tax liabilities do not end with their deaths. Not only do they have to cough up income taxes for their last year of life, but, now that they're dead, new income taxes spring up. And then there is something known generically as transfer taxes. In this chapter, you are going to learn the basic rules governing these death taxes. Don't worry: there is some serious math involved but you are going to let your accountant handle that.

Fiduciary Income Taxes

Remember the Probate Estate you learned about in Chapter 1? In tax law, that's a person. As a person, it is required to pay income taxes. Income tax on what, you ask? Income tax on things like interest from bank accounts, dividends from stocks and mutual funds, rents from real estate, and capital gain from the sale of those things. In short, all of the probate assets that were generating income for the decedents before they died are now owned by the Probate Estate. As a result, the Probate Estate has income and the IRS would like a piece of it.

Remember the Trust Estate you learned about in Chapter 1? That, too, is now a taxable person. Normally, living trusts are not taxable persons so long as they can be revoked. But when the only person who could have revoked it has gone toes up, its status naturally changes. Just as with the Probate Estate, income generated by trust assets are still taxable.

Now the cool thing about Probate Estates and Irrevocable Trusts is that they both get a deduction for any income they pass on to beneficiaries (known as Distributable Net Income or DNI). As a result, the income tax burden actually shifts to the beneficiaries. And that's a good thing since, in most cases, "natural persons" (i.e., taxpayers with 46 chromosomes) pay income tax at a much lower rate. Your accountant will use a computer program to calculate the tax the Probate Estate or Trust Estate would have to pay if income is not distributed and compare it to the likely tax the beneficiaries would have to pay if the income is distributed to them. With your consent, the accountant will then go with the scenario that generates the lowest tax.

Although the accountant prepares the fiduciary income tax returns each year, it is ultimately the responsibility of the executor (Probate Estate) and the trustee (Trust Estate) to file those returns and pay the tax. It's your butt that will be in the legal sling if you don't. And since failure to file returns and pay taxes results in hefty penalties, the beneficiaries will be looking to you to reimburse the estates for the lost cash. You are also responsible for the accuracy of those returns. Accordingly, it is really, really, really important that you hire an accountant who is not just familiar with fiduciary tax returns but one who does them all the time. So if you ask an accountant, "Do you know about DNI?" and the answer is, "Were you arrested for drunk driving?," move on to the next candidate.

Transfer Taxes

The Federal Estate Tax

Tax law is a funny thing. You can spend your entire lifetime creating wealth despite having to share it with the

U.S. Treasury each year and, still, you can owe more tax because you managed to die with too much left over. Sound incredibly unfair? It is. But since tax laws are written by Congressmen and Senators, and since these ladies and gentleman depend on your votes to keep them in gravy, it behooves them to limit the number of voters they subject to an unfair tax. So, although there is a Federal Estate Tax, it only applies to natural persons whose estates total more than $5,430,000. In other words, they chose to offend a really small voting bloc. It's sort of the same reason burglars prefer to hit homes with the most silver instead of every home on the block: biggest gain for the lowest risk.

In keeping with this notion of revenue without repercussion, the number of decedents subject to the tax is reduced still further by eliminating surviving spouses from the group of taxpayers. In other words, if Bill Gates dies tomorrow and leaves everything to his wife, there will be no estate tax. This is known as the Unlimited Marital Deduction. Of course this merely delays—and usually increases—the tax owed when the wife dies but, politically, that is still better than imposing the tax on a spouse.

The Federal Estate Tax can also be eliminated by distributing all of the assets to charity. But whether you can eliminate the tax depends entirely on how the will and trust are written. If the decedent was rich but single and not disposed to making charitable bequests, the only deductions you will be allowed to take are for costs of administration (i.e., all those professionals you will be hiring).

If after taking deductions for gifts to spouse, gift to charities, and costs of administration, your estates still total more than $5,450,000, the tax rate is 40% of the excess. So, for example, if the taxable estate (i.e., the total of your estates less deductions) is $6,450,000, the tax will be $400,000.

Beyond these basic concepts, the Federal Estate Tax, like the Fiduciary Income Tax, is blindingly complex. So, once again, you will leave the preparation of the Federal Estate Tax return to the professional. In some cases, the return is prepared by the accountant. In some cases, the return is prepared by the lawyer. In most cases, however, the two work together to blunt the tax as much as possible.

State Estate Taxes

Just a head's up: Some states also impose an estate tax. Most merely copy the Federal Estate Tax but impose a lower tax rate. And then there are some that are truly unique. Nevertheless, all have one thing in common: They are imposed on the total of the estates. Inheritance taxes work on an entirely different principal.

State Inheritance Taxes

The good news is that there is no federal inheritance tax. The bad news is that there are inheritance taxes at all. I say that because of the rationale behind them. Unlike an estate tax, which punishes the decedent for having been too successful, an inheritance tax punishes the estates' beneficiaries for being too distant a relative or not a relative at all.

For example, let's say you are informed that your rich uncle has just died and left you a million dollars. You are not all that surprised. You were close to your uncle. You visited him regularly to check up on him. You made sure that his bills were paid, his house was clean, and that he was taking all of his medication. You did this mainly because you loved him but also because you knew his son did nothing for him. The irony is that, if your uncle left a million dollars to his son as well, the inheritance tax you pay will be significantly higher than the tax paid by the son. That is because the inheritance tax rates go up the more distantly you are related to the decedent.

It is important to note that laws vary from one state to the next. So the tax disparity between a son and a nephew will be greater or less depending on where the decedent had resided. Some states, like Virginia, don't have an inheritance tax at all. In fact, Virginia has neither an estate tax nor an inheritance tax.

These state transfer taxes (i.e., the state estate tax and the state inheritance tax) all have their own tax return forms. Your accountant will know which form to prepare.

What Your Accountant Needs From You

Fiduciary Income Tax Returns

Yeah, it's great that we have accountants to crunch the numbers for us and wade through all the tax rules and regulations. But you have to supply the raw materials.

So, for example, let's say that your accountant, Bob, is going to prepare this year's fiduciary income tax returns. Bob is depending on you to provide all of those income reporting forms that banks and brokers have been sending to you since the beginning of the year. They are easily recognized by the bold statement on the envelope proclaiming, "IMPORTANT TAX DOCUMENT. DO NOT DESTROY." And they almost always bear the number "1099."

Once Bob knows what kind of cash the Probate Estate and the Trust Estate have been cranking out, he needs to know about all of the expenses you paid last year and what, if any, distributions you made to beneficiaries. Bob will determine which expenses are deductible and how much income is taxable to the beneficiaries.

So your job here is clear: Keep good records. If you're the kind of person who never balances your checkbook and doesn't get the joke, "How can I be overdrawn? I still have checks," you should hire a bookkeeper. Seriously, while there are many people you can afford to tick off, the IRS agent is not one of them. What's more, if you don't give the accountant the needed information and do it in a timely fashion, you just may find yourself without an accountant.

Finally, keep in mind that the accountant may be preparing as many as four annual income tax returns: the federal fiduciary income tax return for the Probate Estate, the state fiduciary income tax return for the Probate Estate, the federal fiduciary income tax return for the Trust Estate, and the state fiduciary income tax return for the Trust Estate. There may also be income tax returns for Ancillary Probate Estates (e.g., rents from real estate in other states). Your job is to make sure that your accountant has prepared all of these returns and, if not, explain why not. Rarely does a good accountant drop the ball but, remember, it's your keister on the line. Be vigilant.

Federal and State Transfer Tax Returns

Whether it's an estate tax or an inheritance tax, the accountant—and often the lawyer—requires the date of death values for all of the assets in all of the four estates. Regardless of the type of estate or the type of transfer tax, those valuations are based on the same federal regulations. Here is how they work:

Real Estate—Appraised value. You must hire an appraiser to give you the property's true value. You cannot rely on the county tax assessment. Assessments can be overvalued because the county simply needs more revenue, or they can be undervalued because they have not been updated for years (sometimes, decades).

Cash—Balance at day's end. It is a small matter to ask the bank for the exact balance of the decedent's cash accounts on the date of death. Keep in mind, however, that a bank may only release that information to an executor if the account is a Probate Estate asset, to a trustee if the account was a Trust Estate asset, or to a joint owner or beneficiary if the account was a Contract Estate asset.

Securities—Average of high and low bids on the date of death. It's OK if you don't know what a bid is. The broker knows. The broker also has software that quickly and effortlessly computes these figures for you faster than you can say, "Why did I take this job?" The same confidentiality rules apply, however. The broker may not divulge this information to you unless you are the executor, trustee, joint-owner, or beneficiary. (If the decedent did not use a broker, you will have to request this information from each company in which the decedent owned stock.)

Life Insurance—Face amount. The face amount is the insurance amount. So, for example, if you take out a $10,000 life insurance policy, $10,000 is the face amount. It is important to distinguish that figure from the proceeds actually paid out. If there is a delay between the decedent's date of death and the payout date (there always is), the payout will include interest the insurance company pays for the time it was holding the face amount for you. (Your accountant will report the interest portion on the appropriate fiduciary income tax return.) Usually, only the beneficiary of the policy can get this information.

Retirement Accounts—Balance at day's end. I'm talking about things like 401(k)s and IRAs. I am not referring to pensions. (Pensions are somewhat antiquated arrangements, whereby an employer continues to pay a retired employee for so long as the retiree shall live. Unlike retirement accounts, pensions die with the retiree.) Usually, only the beneficiary of the retirement account can get this information.

Tangible Personal Property (aka the Knick-Knack Estate)—Valuation depends on whether or not the asset was ever appraised or whether it was insured for a certain value. Otherwise, its value is presumed to be whatever you got when you sold it. If you don't sell it, you can usually ignore it as having little or no value. Don't believe me? Go to an estate auction sometime and see solid silver tea services sell for $20. And that's it. Provide the accountant with those figures and let the calculations commence.

Summing Up

In addition to the decedent's final income tax return, there are five kinds of taxes for which an executor is responsible: federal fiduciary income tax, state fiduciary income tax, federal estate tax, state estate tax, and state inheritance tax. Your accountant will prepare most or all of these returns for you. However, your accountant is dependent on you to provide the needed information in an accurate and timely manner.

Things to Do

1. Interview and select your accountant.
2. Have your accountant obtain Employer Identification Numbers for the Probate Estate and the Trust Estate.
3. Forward all of the decedent's tax information forms to your accountant as soon as you receive them (e.g., W-2, 1099).
4. Prepare a list of the decedent's assets and debts, and provide a copy to both your attorney and your accountant.
5. Promptly provide anything else your accountant requires.

Chapter 6

The Appraiser and Valuation Methods

Why Values Matter

It may seem obvious that executors need to know what their estates are worth. And that is a correct instinct. But the reasons executors need to know precise values is actually more complex. You not only need to put a value on everything, you need to assign values that will be universally accepted. And establishing these universally accepted values is important for four reasons.

1. Fairness—If a will or trust requires that a beneficiary receive an equal share of the estate but does not specify what comprises that share, accurate and accepted values are needed to first calculate the total value of

the share and then to decide how to satisfy that share. Or if the will or trust requires that a beneficiary receive a specific dollar amount but, again, does not instruct you as to how to pay that bequest, you need accurate values to make an equitable distribution. If the entire estate was comprised of cash, this would be an easy problem to solve. Without cash, proper valuations are indispensable.

2. Tax Basis—A rule that is widely known among financial professional but less so among laymen is the Step-Up Basis Rule. The rule is simply this: When someone dies, the cost basis of most of their assets instantly becomes the date of death value. This is important because cost basis is what we use to calculate capital gain. For example, let's say you buy a share of stock at $10 and then sell it for $15, you have a $5 capital gain. And capital gains are taxed. But if you didn't sell it and died when that share was worth $15, the price you were deemed to have paid for it would instantly become $15. If you were to then sell that share for

$15, there would be no capital gain and, therefore, no tax on it. Pretty cool, huh? Knowing what assets are worth when someone dies justifies paying little or no tax when they are later sold.

3. Fiduciary Duty—As an executor or a trustee, you have an obligation to assign values to assets that conform to universally acceptable standards. In short, you don't get to guess.

4. Liability—Your own financial well-being is dependent on the use of universally accepted valuations. For example, let's say that you look at the decedent's last statement from his stock broker. The statement is less than a month old. On that statement, it shows that 100 shares of X Corporation are worth the same as 100 shares of Y Corporation. And let's say that the will or trust instructs you to distribute the stock equally to the decedent's two children. So you give the X Corporation stock to John and the Y Corporation stock to Sue. Sue finds out that, on her father's date of death, the 100 shares of X Corporation was worth

10 times what her Y Corporation stock was worth because, the day before her father died, Y Corporation was named as a defendant in a multi-billion-dollar lawsuit, causing the stock to plummet. Suffice to say that Y Corporation isn't going to be the only one being sued. You have enough to worry about without being sued for malfeasance.

Having said all of this, one rule of accepted valuation is that what something sells for is deemed to be its value. But unless you are selling assets on the decedent's date of death (which is highly unlikely), that value may be higher or lower than the date of death value. And date of death value is the number you are looking for.

The Internal Revenue Service, Probate Courts, and local taxing authorities all agree that the Federal Treasury Regulations for valuing all manner of property are the gold standard. However, those regulations make it clear that one rule does not fit all and that there are very different rules for valuing different kinds of assets. Here we are going to review the rules for valuing the following: (1) real estate, (2) securities (e.g., stocks and bonds), (3) life insurance, (4) cash accounts (e.g., checking, savings, certificates of deposit), (5) businesses, (6) vehicles, and (7) tangible personal property (i.e., the Knick-Knack Estate). I don't expect you to become an appraiser but, just as with selecting an accountant or lawyer, you need to know the rules so that you select and oversee the proper professional.

Real Estate

Homes, vacation homes, and investment real estate (i.e., rental property) are usually the most valuable assets in any estate. They are also the assets with the greatest potential capital gain. For example, my parents purchased their home in 1957 for $25,000. I sold it in 2010 for $250,000. That is a capital gain of $225,000! Had it not been for the Step-Up Basis Rule, their estates would have been liable for over $30,000 in income tax. Had it not been for all the repairs that it required, I could have sold their home for $350,000, resulting in tax in excess of $50,000! But the Basis Step-Up Rule says that their home's basis was equal to its date of death value. Accordingly, it was important that a date of death value was established in a way consistent with the Federal Treasure Regulations and that, in turn, requires the assistance of a licensed real estate appraiser.

More often than not, a licensed real estate appraiser will look to see what comparable homes in the neighborhood have sold for recently (aka Comps). When there are no comparable sales, valuation becomes more complex and appraisers will resort to other methods to reach their opinions. But it is the fact that the appraiser is licensed that is key. And that's because, to be licensed, the appraiser must complete a course of study, work with a licensed appraiser to gain experience, and then pass the state's licensing examination. Accordingly, their opinions are rarely challenged— even by the Internal Revenue Service. In fact, although the Treasury Regulations do not require it, the IRS insists on the opinion of a licensed real estate appraiser before they will accept the value we submit to them on a Federal Estate Tax Return.

In my practice, I come across individuals who actually believe that a home's value is equal to the county's assessment (the value the county uses to calculate real estate tax). Nothing could be farther from the truth. Urban and suburban counties have an immense bias in favor of higher values because the higher the value, the higher the real estate tax. For example, after the real estate market crashed in 2008, one county in Northern Virginia came up with a creative solution to the impending drop in their tax revenue. They acknowledged that the value of houses had dropped but insisted that the value of the land the houses sat upon went up. As a result, assessments—and the resulting real estate taxes—did not decline. It was not a popular decision. Under extreme public pressure, the county later reversed its policy.

On the other hand, in some rural areas of the country, assessments have not changed in decades. Those counties require less revenue and therefore have less motivation to change assessments. As a result, home assessments fall well below their true values. In short, an assessment is never a reliable valuation.

There are, however, informal valuations that are often as reliable as the opinion of a licensed real estate appraiser. The website, Zillow.com, for example, is actually very reliable. Nevertheless, the Internal Revenue Service is taking a wait-and-see approach for now and still insists on the opinion of an actual flesh and blood appraiser.

Securities

One of the treasury's more common-sense rules involves the valuation of stocks and bonds. The rule is that you take the average of the date of death high and low bids on the stock you wish to value. (I said common-sense method of valuation; I didn't say it would make sense to someone who has never traded stocks.) Let's break down the rule for those of you who have no experience with the securities market. A "bid" is the amount of money offered for a single share of stock (usually through a stock exchange like the one in New York). On the date of death, there was a bid that was the highest one that day. Likewise, on the date of death, there was a bid that was the lowest one that day. You simply add the two bids together and divide by two.

For example, let's say that the decedent owned 10 shares of General Motors. On the date of death, the high bid for a single share of stock in General Motors was $51 and the lowest bid was $49. The date of death value of a single share of stock in General Motors, therefore, was $50 ($49 plus $51 equals $100; $100 divided by 2 equals $50). Before the rise of the Internet, this information was only available in print form (e.g., newspapers). Now, however, high and low bids on any date (not just today) can be found in a flash. Of course, even with the aid of computers and websites, if you have a thousand different stocks to value, it's going to take you some time. On the other hand, if the decedent had their stocks with a brokerage, such as Merrill Lynch or Edward Jones, their computers will serve up all of those date of death values faster than you can say, "easy money."

However, only publicly traded stocks are bid upon on a daily basis. Stock in private companies is not for sale on the stock exchange. If the decedent owned stock in such a company, you will need to contact the company directly and ask what they would have paid to redeem the decedent's stock on the date of death. (Some companies are better at this than others.) Often there is an agreement among the stockholders that sets this redemption value. In some cases, the board of directors sets the redemption value at their regular meeting. If a stock is not publicly traded, you will have to make due with one of these alternate methods.

For example, while settling my parents' estates, I came across a small dividend check from a bottled water company in Pennsylvania. The check stub indicated that my father owned 48 shares in his name alone. That is, it was a Probate Estate asset. If those 48 shares were worthless—or even near worthless—I could abandon them and spare myself a probate case. If they had significant value, I was going to have to drive almost 200 miles to my parent's county of residence and be sworn in as executor just to redeem those few shares.

A quick online search confirmed my suspicion that the company's stock was not traded on any stock exchange. So, I looked them up and gave them a call. A very nice woman told me that, at the directors meeting closest to my father's date of death, a value of $48,000 was given to my dad's 48 shares. So, I was off to the Keystone State to become executor.

Life Insurance

You would think something as common-sense as life insurance would be easy to value. The decedent puts down a bet that he is going to die during the term of the insurance and the insurance company bets against him. The premium is the wager and the pre-established death benefit is the payout. Makes sense to any gambler but, unfortunately, it's not quite that simple.

The first question you have to ask yourself is who is the insured? Usually, when executors discover that the decedent owned life insurance, they just assume that the decedent was the one whose life was insured. And, in most cases, they would be right. However, it is also possible to own insurance on the life of someone else. The decedent may have owned insurance on his spouse, for example. Is that worth anything? Again, it all depends.

If the insurance on the spouse is what is known as term life insurance, there is just a death benefit. However, since the spouse is not the one who has died, the policy has no value. On the other hand, some life insurance policies have what is known as a cash value. At any time, the policy can be exchanged (i.e., surrendered) for the cash value. If that is the case, then the policy did have value; the cash value of the policy on the decedent's date of death even though he was not the one insured.

To make this all the more complex, you have to understand that insurance companies don't pay anything on the date of death. There is an entire claims process that must be completed before the life insurance proceeds are paid. The insurance company will want information on the decedent, the policy, and the beneficiary. They will want to know if the beneficiary wants the proceeds paid out in a lump sum, in installments, or, in many cases, held for the beneficiary in a sort of bank account. And, of course, they are going to want proof that there has, in fact, been a death. While this whole process is snaking along, the insurance company is paying interest on the amount that was actually due to the beneficiaries on the date of death but which has not yet been paid. When the check finally arrives, it will not be an even number. So, for example, even though the insurance policy sets the death benefit at $50,000, the check will be larger than that. The excess is the interest. And here we get technical. For while the death benefit is considered an asset of the Contract Estate, the interest is income to the beneficiary. What is the difference you ask? The difference is that the death benefit is subject to death taxes. The interest is subject to income taxes—an important distinction that escapes almost everyone except your accountant and the Internal Revenue Service.

Cash Accounts

As was the case with my grandmother, some people like to have cash on hand. They may keep it in a safe or, like my grandmother, may tape it to the underside of drawers. In such cases, valuation is simple. Add up the money. That is your value. But that's not what we are talking about here. Here we are talking about money held for the decedent by financial institutions such as banks, brokers, and, as we have just seen, life insurance companies.

Cash accounts come in many forms. Most people are familiar with checking and savings accounts but may be less familiar with share accounts, money market accounts, and certificates of deposit. It doesn't really matter. They are all essentially loans to the financial institutions and those institutions pay interest in return (although not in every case). All you need to do to value a cash account is to call the bank, broker, or insurance company and ask for the balance in each account at close of business on the date of death. Those are your values. However, just as with life insurance, these accounts continue to generate interest after the date of death. And, just like life insurance, the balance in the account at the close of business on the date of death is an asset. The interest earned since then is income. Assets are subject to death taxes. Interest is only subject to income taxes.

Businesses

The vast majority of Americans don't own a business. However, there are still a lot who do. If your decedent owned a business, it is very important that you understand two things: (1) the business must be accurately valued, and (2) you are not going to be the one to do it. Methods of business valuation are numerous, extraordinarily complex, and well beyond the scope of this book. So, just as with real estate, you are going to need a business appraiser.

On the other hand, it is possible to establish a value for the business in advance and, if not done in an abusive manner, the IRS will accept it. The technique is called valuation by Buy-Sell Agreement. In short, any time before the business owner dies, he may enter into an agreement with a prospective buyer (usually a partner or employee). The purchase price of the business, as set forth in the agreement, becomes its value.

There are two kinds of Buy-Sell Agreements: funded and unfunded. An unfunded agreement does not tell you how the buyer is paying for the business. A funded agreement, on the other hand, identifies the source of the purchase money. In such cases, the purchase money is almost always provided by life insurance. That is, the life of the business owner is insured for the same amount of money as the purchase price of the business. There are two advantages to this arrangement. First, the sale is not dependent on the buyer coming up with the cash. And, second, the executor now has additional liquidity to pay the decedent's bills. For these reasons, Funded Buy-Sell Agreements are extremely popular and very common. So, before hiring an appraiser, thoroughly review the decedent's business records and interview all employees and partners. If there is a Buy-Sell Agreement in place, an appraiser won't be needed. The business's value will be the purchase price established by the agreement.

However, remember I said that the IRS would accept the Buy-Sell Agreement valuation method provided that it was not used in an abusive fashion. To the IRS, any method of valuation that promotes "form over substance" is abusive. Accordingly, a Buy-Sell Agreement, funded or not, that sets the selling price at $1 is abusive and will be disallowed. Of course, the business may only be worth a dollar but the burden of proof is on the executor.

In the absence of proof, the IRS has the prerogative to value the business themselves. And although the rank and file of IRS staff is comprised of poorly trained accountants, they are by no means qualified appraisers. In fact, there have been many cases where the IRS used the "capitalization method" to value small businesses. The capitalization method is best illustrated by asking, "At today's interest rates, how much would an asset have to be worth to generate a given amount of gross revenue?" So, for example, if a small business grosses $100,000 per year and current interest rates are 1%, then the business must be worth a hundred times $100,000 or $10 million! Don't be shocked. Such nuttiness is the norm for the IRS. So, make no mistake: In the absence of a Buy-Sell Agreement, you will need a qualified appraiser.

Vehicles

Cars are easy to value. Simply consult a publication known as the Kelley Blue Book (aka The Blue Book). There you will find values for virtually every car ever made. Each car will have three values: retail, private party, and trade. Retail is the price that a used car dealer would ask for the car. Private party is the price you could ask if you put the car out on the lawn with a "For Sale" sign on the windshield. And trade is the credit a dealership would give you if you bought a new car and used the decedent's car as part of the payment. These values are usually within a few thousand dollars of each other. And, since the vast majority of used cars are not worth all that much, the Internal Revenue Service really doesn't care which value you use. Officially, they prefer to see the private sale value. But, having said that, even they won't haggle over the few dollars difference between the retail value and the trade value on a 1972 Plymouth Duster.

When it comes to other vehicles, from airplanes to lawn tractors, things become a little less clear. In the absence of a clearly detailed valuation method (e.g., average high-low bid for stocks) the treasury regulations lean toward fair market value. Fair market value simply means what you can sell it for. This is also known as "passing the buck." At some point, the drafters of the treasury regulations simply threw up their hands and said, "We can't come up with an arbitrary value for everything! Figure it out for yourselves!" So there you have it. When it comes to vehicles other than cars, it's all on you. In such cases, you have two choices: (1) make an educated guess, or (2) sell the vehicle. The IRS may take exception to your educated guess and, if it means more money for the treasury, trust me, they will. But, remember, the selling price of anything within a year of the date of death is presumptively its true fair market value. Just remember that transferring a title to a mint-condition World War II P51 Mustang fighter plane to your brother-in-law in exchange for a case of beer will be considered "form over substance" and summarily disallowed.

Tangible Personal Property

Just to refresh your memory, tangible personal property is what makes up the Knick-Knack Estate. It is anything with intrinsic value, no matter how little that value might be. For the most part, the IRS proceeds on the assumption that if you haven't insured an item, it can't be worth very much. Therefore, an insured engagement ring will need to be valued at its insured value. On the other hand, if an engagement ring was not insured because it can be replaced with a quarter and a gum ball machine, it can be exempted from valuation.

This can be problematic if your decedent carried insurance on an item that was once valuable but is now near worthless. For example, my father loved cameras. For decades he bought one after another after another and dutifully insured them for the purchase price. However, he failed to recognize the affect that superior digital photography had on the value of film cameras. As a result, he always renewed his insurance policies for the same values (and, disturbingly, his insurance agent let him). I was forced to itemize each and every one of his film cameras on his Federal Estate Tax Return per its insurance valuation. Of course, had he not specifically bequeathed the cameras to one of my brothers, I could have sold them (assuming I could find a buyer) and, in so doing, established their true values.

Of course the bulk of the tangible personal property will be only slightly north of worthless. Nevertheless, the executor has a duty to liquidate any tangible personal property that is not specifically bequeathed to someone. Whether you sell it at an auction, through the want ads, to a business that buys estate jewelry, or even to a pawn shop, what you get for it is the fair market value.

Summing Up

Universally accepted valuation of the decedent's assets is important for four reasons: fairness to the beneficiaries, establishing a tax basis, meeting your fiduciary duty, and protecting yourself from lawsuits. The method of valuation varies with the nature of the asset. Real estate value is most often established by a licensed appraiser. Stocks and bonds are valued using the average high-low bid method. Life insurance is usually the stated death benefit even though the proceeds you receive may be partly interest. Cash accounts with banks are the account balances at the close of business on the date of death. Businesses, as with real estate, require the opinion of a licensed appraiser. The value of cars is established by a book such as the Kelley Blue Book. And, finally, tangible personal property is valued at either its insured value or sale proceeds.

Things to Do

1. Update your list of assets and debts using the accepted and proper valuations.
2. Provide a copy of your list to both your lawyer and your accountant.

Chapter 7

The Auctioneer and the Trash Man

As you recall from Chapter 1, every decedent leaves a Knick-Knack Estate. It encompasses furniture, jewelry, clothing, books, appliances, and, yes, even knick-knacks. Anything that has value in and of itself—no matter how little—is part of the Knick-Knack Estate. Almost always the least valuable estate, it is often the most challenging to administer, as you will see.

The technical term for knick-knacks is tangible personal property and is easily distinguished from intangible personal property, which merely represents value somewhere else. For example, cash, stocks, and bonds are, in and of themselves, worthless paper but have value as representations of currency, corporate assets, and debt.

The line between the two kinds of personal property is not always clear, however, and occasionally you will come across items that are both tangible and intangible. United States coins minted before 1965, for example. Before 1965, coins were made primarily from silver so that a quarter from 1964 is now worth more than a quarter. We will return to the issue of coins later in the chapter.

Your first task is to identify the tangible personal property, which is a rather simple matter. Your next task is a bit more difficult. You have to divide the tangible personal property into three groups. Think of them as three piles of stuff. The first pile consists of those items that are promised to or desired by someone; we will call these items the Heirloom Pile. The second pile is made up of items that nobody wants but which can be sold; we will call these items the Auctionables Pile. The third pile is everything that's left over; the worthless and the unwanted, which we will call the Junk Pile. You will find that this last pile is usually the biggest one, but it is the easiest one to handle.

So, for example, let's say that the decedent left some antique furniture, some valuable jewelry, some costume jewelry, and a safe filled with cash and stock certificates. The cash and stock certificates are intangible personal property and, therefore, not part of the Knick-Knack Estate. You will handle them differently as we shall see in a later chapter. The remaining items are tangible personal property. Let's assume that the will left some of the valuable jewelry to the decedent's child. It is your duty, of course, to distribute items in accordance with the will. Having done that, you may offer all of the remaining items to the beneficiaries of the Probate Estate. Let's say they choose the remaining valuable jewelry, some of the furniture, and the safe but nothing else. This is the Heirloom Pile. After such heirlooms, keepsakes, and mementos are distributed, you will attempt to identify those items that can be sold, privately or at auction. To do that will most likely require the assistance of an auctioneer. (More about auctions and auctioneers later.) This is your Auctionables Pile. Now you are left with, say, the costume jewelry and the bulk of the furniture. That is your Junk Pile. Now let's talk about how to dispense with each pile. After that, we will review your duties and costs associated with each pile.

Disposition

The Heirloom Pile

In theory, distributing items of personal property to people who want them should be simple. And sometimes it is, like when there is only one beneficiary or the will specifies which item goes to which beneficiary. Usually, that is not the case, however. You are most likely going to have to referee disputes between grown individuals—usually siblings—who cannot agree upon who is to get what. There are several methods you can suggest to them.

The most common method of distribution is having the beneficiaries take turns. You secure a pair of dice and have each interested person roll the dice. Whoever rolls the highest number goes first and may select one item. The person who rolls the second highest number goes next, and so forth. After everyone has made a selection, the process repeats until all items that are desired have been selected.

The problem with such a method of distribution should be obvious. The persons who selects first may choose the most valuable items. As a result, the distribution may be inherently unfair. Many times the inequity is not discovered until much, much later.

For example, I know of two sisters who were dividing their mother's jewelry. The older and more aggressive of the two declared that she should go first since she was older (a unique although arbitrary thought process). The more diminutive sister agreed. The older sister then selected a ring containing a 2-carat diamond. The younger sister selected a ring with a much smaller diamond. The value of the remaining jewelry wound up being divided roughly equally. Years passed and the older sister took her ring to a jeweler to have it reset. The jeweler asked why she would want to reset a worthless stone. As it turned out, the 2-carat diamond was actually a cubic zirconium. The irony was compounded when the younger sister had her ring appraised and found that the stone was flawless and quite valuable.

Another method of distribution is to poll the beneficiaries separately to find out what each would like to have. Frequently, each beneficiary wants something different and problems are avoided. The "taking turns" approach, on the other hand, seems to promote rivalry, with one person choosing an item for no other reason than that another person wants it. If, however, after polling each beneficiary, there is an item desired by more than one of them, you can broker a deal between them. Perhaps one will relinquish her claim in return for a little more cash. A deal can always be made. The obvious advantage to this method of distribution is that you keep conflict to a minimum rather than promote it.

There is yet another method of distribution that I hesitate to mention because it can lead to unexpected results. It is best demonstrated by an actual case that took place decades ago. The story goes that an elderly woman paid a visit to her lawyer. She told him that she wanted a will that said that every item in her home was to pass to her children "as it is tagged." On her way home, will in hand, she stopped at an office supply store and bought a bag of little yellow tags. She then wrote the names of each child on the tags so that were was a pile of tags for each of her eight children. Then she hung the tags on everything in her home. It was a sea of yellow tags.

Now the reason she did this was because she fought with her children constantly. Being a frugal women, however, she did not want to have to pay her lawyer each time she wanted to disinherit one of the kids. But, with her tag system, after a falling out, she simply moved the tags around. As a result, at least one child was always "in the drawer." The problem arose when she died. The child who was "in the drawer" at the time sued the estate on the grounds that the mother had revoked her will. The revocation took place the first time she attempted to amend her will without the benefit of witnesses and notary as the state required; that is, the first time she moved the tags. The court found in favor of the child, and the woman's entire estate went into intestacy proceedings, giving the child a one-eighth share.

As a result of this case, many states passed legislation that allows for the will to reference a list or tag system that may be changed without revoking the will. Nonetheless, these laws vary from state to state and some states don't have them at all. So, while a list or tag system is fine, if it is referenced in the will, you may be in for a fight.

If all else fails, you as the executor have the power to distribute items any way you see fit. Or, in the alternative, you may simply not distribute anything at all. The beneficiaries must know you have this authority from the outset. It is a sort of a "don't make me turn this car around" kind of threat. It is also possible that the decedent left a list that sets forth who gets what although the list is not mentioned in the will. Such a list is not binding because it is not a will, but it serves to enhance your legal authority and spares you accusations of favoritism or arbitrary action.

Finally, you cannot sanction anyone's claim that the decedent had "promised" them a particular item. Claims such as "Mother always wanted me to have her pearl necklace" or "Dad said I was getting the coin collection" are recited, repeated, and, I believe more often than not, fabricated on an annoyingly consistent basis. They have no legal merit.

The Auctionables Pile

Having dispensed with all of the wanted what-nots, you need to sell what you can. An executor's duty includes maximizing the value of the estate by any prudent and legal means. This begins with hiring an auctioneer.

First, be certain that all of the remaining items are available for inspection. Empty safe deposit boxes, cabinets, and safes. The auctioneer will visit the location or locations where the items are located and begin to identify those things he thinks he can sell. It is not uncommon for this process to be pleasingly informal, with the auctioneer moving from room to room pointing to items as he says, "we can sell that, we can sell that, that's junk, that's crap, that's totally worthless, we can sell that . . ." All the while, an assistant is labeling the items that have been selected for auction.

Once this process is complete, it will probably be your duty to arrange for transportation of the marked items to the auction house. Once there, these items may be sold at a live auction, an online auction, or both.

The auctioneer will take a percentage of the proceeds from the sale of each item. This is the auctioneer's commission. The commission (i.e., the percentage) will vary depending on the nature of the item. Furnishings may be one rate while jewelry is another rate. The rates, as well as other terms of your agreement with the auctioneer, are established by contract prior to the auction. Items that do not sell may be returned to you or sent to the landfill. Again, your contract will specify the disposition of "leftovers."

Of course, if you don't want to pay commissions, you can sell these items yourself. One tried and true method to do this is to hold an estate sale at the decedent's home. (An estate sale is a fancy term for a decedent's yard sale.) You can apply price tags to each item or you can merely accept whatever is offered. What is unsold at the end of the day can be hauled off as junk.

This disadvantage of an estate sale is that you do so blindly since you may have no idea what the items are actually worth. I knew a woman and her mother who were the Genghis and Kubla Khans of estate sales. After a hard day of plundering, they would return home laden with such things as solid-silver trays and tea sets for which they had paid $25 at most. An auctioneer, on the other hand, experienced in the sale of estate property, will often start the bidding with a minimum price that is perhaps more reasonable—not to mention that bidding, in and of itself, can drive up the price.

Or imagine this: Your father is given a painting of some cows standing in a field. The painting itself appears to have water damage—as if someone had dusted it with a fire hose. The ornate frame is cracked in several places and it appears to be beyond repair. Your father puts this homage to heifers in the closet with plans of, someday, having it restored. Then your father dies. Nobody in the family wants the painting and it appears to you that nobody would ever actually pay good money for a bovine family portrait. So you throw it out.

The story is true; all except the part about throwing it out. Luckily, that didn't happen. One Christmas, a friend of my father came to visit. As he was hanging his coat in the closet, he noticed the cow painting. He turned and said to my father, "Carl, I think this is a Bingham. And, if it is, it is worth a great deal of money." My father's friend just happened to be the curator of the Fine Arts Museum of Philadelphia. As it turned out, the painting was indeed genuine and one of three Binghams that had been missing for over 100 years. The museum agreed to restore the painting for free provided they could display it. It later appraised for $850,000. I often wake up in a sweat dreaming I put the Guernsey's out with the trash one Monday morning. An auctioneer reduces the possibility of such a catastrophe.

Assuming I have not yet convinced you to use an auctioneer, you can always place ads online or in local newspapers listing the items and containing the phrase, "Best Offer." This is not the most efficient method of sale, but it is usually quite cheap. The disadvantage to ads, however, is it could take days, weeks, or months before you sell what can be sold. All the while, you will be responsible for all of this stuff.

And this brings us to the issue of one of your most important fiduciary obligations, safekeeping. You have a duty to preserve the knick-knacks with the same fervor as you would a stock portfolio. When it comes to tangible personal property, you are expected to house it and insure it pending sale of it. Since you are most likely storing it in the decedent's home, you will need to be certain that the home is secure. That means changing locks and installing a security system. Furthermore, so long as the home is housing all of this stuff, you can't sell the home. For this reason, which-ever method of sale is fastest is preferred. And the fast-est method of sale is through the auctioneer.

The Junk Pile

Your journey through knick-knack land is coming to an end. All that's left to do is dispose of the remaining tangible personal property—the things that nobody wanted and which could not be sold. Now is the time to call the trash man.

While it is possible to put a limited number of items out on trash day, it is probably impossible, impractical, or illegal to drag a house full of junk to the curb and expect the municipal trash collectors to dispose of it for you. No, you are going to have to hire someone who hauls junk. However, even though we are talk-ing about trash, you want someone who is not going to take out a window while taking out the ottoman. It is therefore prudent to use a referral service such as Angie's List or HomeAdvisor to find someone who is insured, bonded, and has positive reviews.

In the case of my own parents' estates, with the aid of an online review service, I hired a local business that consisted of one man and his sweet and affable daughter—the strongest woman I have ever met. I was not disappointed. I watched the two of them hoist a baby grand piano on their shoulders and march it out the front door. Then went the complete contents of the rest of the house, including a 300-pound TV. They did it all in half a day. The house was empty, and I was able to begin the process of selling it.

Vehicles

Vehicles are a unique type of tangible personal property because they have been registered with the state. Unlike all of the other stuff you have to distribute, distributing a vehicle requires the assistance of a state agency. Variously known as the Department of Motor Vehicles, the Motor Vehicle Administration, or the Motor Vehicle Commission (to name just a few), this agency registers, licenses, and tracks all manner of things with wheels and/or motors. To distribute a car to a person, the executor is going to have to visit the local branch of this agency and present at least two things: (1) the executor's certificate, and (2) the prospective new owner. It is not a complicated process, but it is richly bureaucratic. Each state has its forms and procedures. I strongly recommend that you go to the agency website or call them before you pay a visit. Although, even these proactive steps do not always make the process any smoother.

One way to avoid the problem is to convince the family that nobody really needs the decedent's 1971 Plymouth Duster with 210,000 miles on it. If you can do that then you can donate the car to any number of charities that are more than happy to come and tow it away. All you need is the document that indicates that the decedent owned the car (i.e., the "title"), which you sign over to the charity. Don't have that document? Well then, I'm sorry to say, it's back to the Department of Motor Vehicles to get a replacement. Nothing simple is ever easy.

Of course it is possible that the decedent owned a very valuable vehicle. I'm not talking about your run-of-the-mill Mercedes or BMW. No, I'm referring to something more along the line of a Lamborghini

Diablo or a McLaren Spider—cars that cost a quarter of a million dollars or more. In that case, you are most likely going to have to enlist the aid of the auctioneer to get as much money for the vehicle as possible. That is your job after all: to protect and preserve the estate. Unless such a car was specifically bequeathed to someone, simply giving it away is not an option.

Proceeds

So what do you do with the proceeds of auctions and sales? You are going to have to account for them, so you will need a bank account in which they can be deposited. You cannot use the decedent's bank account. Any bank accountant that the decedent owned must be closed. Rather, you are going to have to open a new bank account in the name of the Probate Estate and use the estate's newly acquired Federal ID Number to do so. Preferably, this should be a checking account since you will eventually need to distribute this money to the beneficiaries. In the good old days, you had an obligation to find a bank that payed the highest interest on checking accounts. These days, however, since checking accounts pay little or no interest, simply use the bank that is most convenient.

Summing Up

The Knick-Knack Estate is composed of the decedent's tangible personal property. These are things that have value in and of themselves, however little value that may be. They can be thought of as fitting into one of three groups: The Heirloom Pile, The Auctionables Pile, and the Junk Pile. The Heirloom Pile is comprised of items that at least one of the beneficiaries wants. The Auctionables Pile consists of remaining items that an auctioneer feels can be sold at auction. What's left is the Junk Pile. You will most likely need to employ someone who hauls junk for a living to dispose of the Junk Pile. Finally, the proceeds of any sale must be deposited into an estate checking account for later distribution.

Things to Do

1. Poll the beneficiaries to see who wants which item of personal property and then determine the best method of distribution to them.

2. Using a review and referral service, select the following members of your team: auctioneer, movers, and trash hauler.

3. Distribute the agreed personal property to the beneficiaries.

4. Use the movers to send the auctionables to your auctioneer.

5. Have the Junk Pile hauled away.

6. Open a checking account for the Probate Estate.

7. Plan your visit to the Department of Motor Vehicles if there are any vehicles.

Chapter 8

Know Your Bureaucrat

Technically, a bureaucrat is any government official. But, in its more colloquial or pejorative use, it refers to any inflexible, low-level government official who extolls the rules over public service. So, technically, the president of the United States is a bureaucrat. But in practice, the term is more likely to refer to the grim-looking person behind the counter at the Department of Motor Vehicles; the one who returns your registration application because your Social Security number is missing a dash. For our purposes, however, it means any person, in any organization, business, or government office, who processes paper. They may, in fact, be the sourpuss at the DMV or they may be the pleasant and helpful branch manager at your local bank. Either way, the simple fact is that you need these people. So be nice.

Government Bureaucrats

Internal Revenue Service

Nothing strikes fear into the hearts of man and woman as the acronym "IRS." Quite possibly the most powerful and influential bill collector on the planet, the IRS benefits from a reputation that is largely undeserved. That is because not all IRS agents are the same, nor do they even share the same job. The IRS is, in fact, comprised of numerous sub-offices; each is staffed by a different sort of bureaucrat. For our purposes, we are going to look at the big four: Processing, Audit, Collection, and Criminal.

It is unlikely that you will ever have official contact with someone who works for Processing. These are the folk who actually process and oversee most of the paper submitted to the Internal Revenue Service in the form of income tax returns. It is a grueling and thankless task. In one case, which the commissioner of the Internal Revenue Service vehemently denied, the staff at the Philadelphia processing center claimed that they were so overwhelmed that they had started hiding tax returns in the suspended ceilings just so that they could claim that they had completed their workload. I am from Philadelphia and I know Philadelphians. If you're like me, the story is *very* believable. In any case, there is no direct contact between taxpayer and processor. These bureaucrats toil in anonymity and are no threat to anyone.

Auditors, on the other hand, are the IRS employees you are most likely to meet face to face. Their job, in a nutshell, is to ensure that what you have entered on your tax return is true, accurate, and in compliance with the Internal Revenue Code and Treasury Regulations. Contrary to popular perception, however, it has been my experience that most are not "out to get you." If you are selected for audit, the audit may be nothing more than a letter requesting additional information about your tax return. And, then again, you may actually be asked to appear at a local IRS office for a more thorough review. Such an audit can be scary but, in all my years of accompanying clients to these "in-person audits," I have never once met with an auditor who seemed angry, aggressive, or unfair. The only problem with auditors, in my opinion, is that most are poorly trained and don't seem to have enough knowledge of the law to do their jobs correctly. More than once, I have had to take a case to the Internal Revenue Service's Appeals Office just so that I could work with someone who was better educated. My point is that, unless you have been dishonest, an audit is nothing to fear.

And then there are the Collection officers. A Collection officer's job is to collect taxes by any means possible. What kind of people are they? How shall I put this? In my experience, Collection officers are a curious combination of Barney Fife and Mad Max. That is to say that they are well aware that they have the power to seize almost anything you own and they find that stimulating. Their knowledge of tax law is poor to say the least. But that doesn't seem to bother them. They simply don't care; nor are they required to. However, before breaking into a cold sweat at the prospect of losing the estate you have been dutifully shepherding, there are two points to keep in mind.

First, if you are in the presence of a Collection officer it is either because you have refused to pay your taxes or, more likely, because you have ignored the auditor's request for information. When you ignore an IRS request for information, the government is well within its rights to assess a tax against you based on the information that is available. And once a tax is assessed against you, the case is turned over to a Collection officer.

Second, even though you have been negligent in dealing with the IRS, you can still seek a court injunction to stop the Collection officer's attempts to seize property. This involves hiring an attorney to go to court for you. Of course, for your attorney to prevail, the Collection officer's actions must have been unlawful (which is certainly not outside the realm of possibility) and the judge must be fair (not always the case), but still, going to court is better than submissively baring your throat. My point is that you always have options. On the other hand, if you are doing your job as executor, it should never get to this point.

The last IRS bureaucrat who may become involved with your decedent's estate is an agent of the Criminal Enforcement Division. These are the agents who carry guns. They are, essentially, the Internal Revenue Service police force. Most taxpayers will only meet with one or more of these agents during a seizure of home or business. Surprisingly, they are not there to seize anything (that is reserved for the jubilant Collection Officers). No, they are there to keep the peace. In my three decades of practice, I have only met one Criminal Enforcement agent and, quite frankly, I found her charming. The only other time you are likely meet a Criminal Enforcement agent is if you have knowingly defrauded the IRS. Don't do that.

State Taxing Authority

It should come as no surprise that tax collection at the state level mirrors tax collection at the federal level. Every state has an agency comparable to the Internal Revenue Service. Most are not nearly as sophisticated, well-funded, or well-manned as the Internal Revenue Service and most are not nearly as aggressive in exercising their mission. Nevertheless, your accountant should be just as well-versed in dealing with state taxing authorities as he is in dealing with the IRS. If not, you may just find yourself fighting a two-front war.

Department of Motor Vehicles

Here's your problem. Your decedent owned a car and, to make matters worse, he owned it in his name alone. Why is this a problem? Well, while most states provide many online services, transferring a title to a vehicle to someone else usually requires a trip to the Department of Motor Vehicles. In addition to the notorious wait times at most DMV offices, you will need to know, in advance, whether this DMV office is going to require a probate certificate.

Some states have enacted legislation that allows someone to take a title to a car without formal probate procedures. Virginia, for example, has had one such law on its books for decades. It says simply that vehicles can be re-titled to the decedent's next of kin without probate. Sounds straightforward, right? It is. The problem is that the vast majority of DMV personnel in Virginia have: (1) never heard of the law, (2) don't care to familiarize themselves with the law, and (3) don't know what a next of kin is. And why should they? As they are quick to remind you, they are not lawyers. For them, the law is whatever their manager says it is. And often, their manager doesn't know the law either.

It seems excessive to enter full-blown probate just to transfer a title to a 1972 Plymouth Duster. So much so that you may be tempted to remove the license plates, tear off the VIN, and abandon the clunker on the side of the road. In fact, executors have been suggesting that to me for years. But, well, no. Don't abandon hope quite yet. Many states have a form of probate that doesn't require all of those pesky inventories and accountings and other filings that stretch a simple job into a year or more. The law in those states provides that probate estates worth less than a given value (e.g., $50,000) may use an affidavit in which the affiant claims, under oath (i.e., notarized), that he or she is entitled to the car. All the executor has to do is record the will with the local probate office. I find that DMV personnel are familiar with these laws.

So why do the employees of the DMV recognize one law and not another? I can't be certain, but I suspect it has something to do with the fact that one law doesn't require a piece of paper and the other does. And, in any bureaucracy, it really is all about the paper. Which means that if your state doesn't recognize either type of law, the paper you are going to need is a probate certificate and that means full-blown probate—for a car.

Which brings me back to your original dilemma: How do you know what your DMV requires? Of course, you can simply call them and ask but that is a little like calling the IRS. You will get an answer but there is a really good chance that it won't be the right one. And if you think that you will get any traction with the old argument, "But I called!" trust me, you won't. So here is what you do: Take the car title as well as your prospective new owner to the DMV and wait your turn. One way or another, you are going to find out what they want. If no other paperwork is required, great. If they use the affidavit system, they usually have a form you can fill out there and then. If probate is your only option, you're just going to have to suck it up. But be nice. Remember that, for a bureaucrat, tantrums are never persuasive and you may well have to deal with this same person on your return. Don't make a bad situation worse.

It's also useful to understand that, just like people, DMV offices are not created the same. Many years ago, I had a client who would visit all of the local DMV offices on a weekly basis, just to see which had the shortest lines and the most helpful employees. (He had a lot of time on his hands.) And then he would call me and give me his findings for the week. Given this insider knowledge, I could advise my executors accordingly. So, if your decedent lived somewhere with numerous DMV offices, ask around. Get a referral, so to speak.

Finally, it bears mentioning that, if the decedent owned a vehicle with another person, and that person is still living, you're off the hook. It is the responsibility of the surviving owner to visit the DMV and remove the decedent's name from the title. (This usually requires little more than a death certificate.) The vehicle is part of the Contract Estate and may have to be reported on the Estate Tax Return as joint property but that is the extent of your involvement. Having said this, it would be prudent of you to examine the title. The following words must appear for this to work: "Joint With Right of Survivorship" or the abbreviation, "JWROS." If the title is silent in this regard, you may be required to probate half a car. Don't laugh. I had just such a case.

Court

Let us assume for a moment that your decedent had assets that must be probated (i.e., assets owned in the decedent's name alone without a beneficiary). Most probate offices are physically located in the county's court of record (the high court of the county). This building also usually houses the land records office. You will probably need their assistance as well. Chances are that you will not need an appointment to visit land records, but you almost always need an appointment to begin the probate process. You attorney should make the appointment for you.

But first things first. Almost all court buildings these days employee security guards and metal detectors at each entrance. Unless you are an attorney who has been pre-cleared by that county's security officials, you are going to have to get in line with everyone else and wait to be screened. The experience is not unlike security checkpoints at the airport. And like airport security, you will need to empty your pockets and place the contents into those little plastic bowls for inspection. Also like airport security, arguing with the officer will not make your day go any better. In addition, many courts do not permit you to carry a cell phone into the building. Some will hold it for you until you are ready to leave but others will not, forcing you to trek back to your car and leave it there. In short, the day you visit the court, for whatever reason, just leave behind any and all metal objects, cell phones, and, of course, weapons (do I really need to tell you this?). Then just be nice.

Once you have located the probate office, your attorney will have to make your presence known. While some of the more populous counties have a receptionist and a sign-in procedure, others counties require that you waive your arms and repeat "excuse me" until someone actually notices you. Once, in a very rural county, after much arm waiving, I discovered that the probate office was actually a broom closet behind the main desk and that the only probate clerk was on her cigarette break. To borrow a rule from the game of golf, you play them as they lay.

The probate clerk's job is to "qualify" you as the executor of the estate. The clerk will need to see an original death certificate and, if there is one, the original will. You will be asked the names and locations of your decedent's next of kin (spouse, children, etc.), and you will be asked about the types and values of the probate assets (securities, cash accounts, etc.). Your attorney should have obtained from you both the documents and the needed information prior to your visit. You will then be required to give your personal bond (i.e., a promise that if any assets turn up missing on your watch, you will replace them). In some instances (e.g., you are from out of state), you may be required to purchase "surety" from a local bondsman (i.e., insurance to protect the estate from your presumably nefarious nature). Once all the paperwork is completed, you will be asked to raise your right hand and swear that you will fulfill your duties as executor. At this point, your job has just begun. However, in the vast majority of cases, you will not be seeing the probate clerk ever again.

While you are at the courthouse, your attorney may need to drop by the land records office. Land records is the repository of every deed for every piece of property in the county. If your decedent owned real estate, your attorney will need to obtain a copy of the deed so that a new one can be prepared, transferring the property to a buyer or to a beneficiary. Obtaining a deed is a simple matter. Your attorney need only ask for the last deed in the chain of title for a particular address. The clerk then prints out the copy from a computer database (although some less affluent counties still rely on using the original deed and a copy machine).

Your interaction with the land records clerk will be brief and nothing like the hour you just spent with the probate clerk. But, on occasion, it can actually be entertaining. Decades ago, when I was a very young lawyer, I went to the land records office in a very rural Virginia county. When I walked in, I saw long shelves of books on one side of the room and a very long counter on the other side. Near me but behind the counter was an elderly, gray-haired woman. We were the only persons in the room. She looked at me and said, "May I help you, young man?" Not certain if I was in the right place, I replied, "Deeds?" She pointed to the shelves of books containing all of the county's deeds.

I said, "No. I need to record a deed." She pointed to the far end of the counter. So I walked to the far end of the counter. And so did she. When we both arrived there, she turned toward me, looked me in the eye, and said, "May I help you, young man?" It was a surreal moment. To this day, I don't know if she was "funnin" me, suffering short-term memory loss, or more likely I think, just being a bureaucrat.

Private Bureaucrats

Insurance Companies

The difference between a government bureaucrat and a private one can be subtle or profound. Nowhere is this premise better illustrated than with life insurance companies. When you attempt to make a claim for the decedent's life insurance, you may be tempted to call the company's 800 number. However, while the person who answers the 800 number is ostensibly there to help you, they are frequently not all that helpful. To be fair, these people have a job that requires them to take countless calls from confused, desperate, and often belligerent customers on a daily basis. And that can take its toll. If they are very, very good at their job, they maintain a pleasant and professional demeanor as they assist you with your questions and claims. My experience, however, is that they often seem unable to assist you and become belligerent and dismissive when confronted with your frustration (e.g., "Well, I'm sorry, sir, but there is simply nothing I can do"). And that is really not all that surprising. People need an incentive to do their jobs well. So the rule of thumb is that, rather than call the 800 number, you simply locate your decedent's agent.

An insurance agent is, in fact, an independent contractor and not an employee of the insurance company. The agent's business deal with the insurance company is that if he successfully signs you up for a life insurance policy, he gets a part of the premiums you pay. A good insurance salesman can make a rather tidy living, receiving what amounts to royalties on policies sold to customers years and years ago, but only so long as the customers continue to pay the premiums. As a result, an insurance agent has a vested interest in your happiness in a way that someone paid by the hour to answer the phone does not. So, whenever you discover that your decedent had life insurance, the rule of thumb is to first determine if there is an agent, then dispose of the 800 number, and then call the agent.

All of the major insurance companies contract with agents to sell their products. However, it is possible that your decedent bought life insurance after viewing a late-night TV commercial. You know the kind. The one with such breathless pitches as, "You can get 10, 20 . . . up to 50,000 dollars in terms life insurance with no medical exam! And your premiums will never go up!" More about such insurance in a later chapter, but suffice to say there is no agent. You will be calling an 800 number.

You may also discover that your decedent had insurance through work, even if the decedent had retired long ago. If the employment was in the private sector, you simply need to call the employer. If it is a large employer (e.g., IBM, Microsoft) you will be put in touch with a department known as Human Resources or the like. They will then walk you through the claims process. If your decedent worked for the state or local government, you will be handed off to a similar department. But if your decedent worked for the federal government, you will need to call the Office of Personal Management, or OPM. If that is the case, you will be entering a whole new level of bureaucracy and you may need the assistance of your attorney.

Bankers

At the moment of death, your decedent's taxable entity disappeared. Or, to put it another way, the decedent's final income tax return will be for a year that began on January 1 and ended on the date of death. And that is because the Social Security number was retired like an old football jersey—never to be used by anyone ever again. In its place, up to two new taxable entities sprang into existence: the Probate Estate and the Trust Estate.

The Probate Estate, as you may recall, is any asset that the decedent owned in his own name alone with no beneficiary named. If your decedent had probate assets, then the accumulation of those assets is a taxable entity and one for which you will have to file annual income tax returns until the Probate Estate has been distributed. As a taxable entity, it is going to require an Employer Identification Number (EIN).

The Trust Estate is the accumulation of assets held in the name of the decedent's previously revocable living trust. But since he was the only person who could have revoked the trust, the trust is now irrevocable and irrevocable trusts are also taxable entities requiring annual income tax return filings. It is going to require an EIN as well.

What does all of this have to do with the banker? Well, in short, the Probate Estate is going to require at least a checking account and the bank will not be able to open that account without an EIN. The same is true for any bank accounts that were held in the name of the living trust. They will all have to be closed and new bank accounts opened with the trust's new EIN. So, before dropping by your decedent's bank or credit union, you are going to have to go the Internal Revenue Service website to obtain these numbers. Getting the EIN numbers is usually the accountant's job, but if you are pressed for time or you have not as yet hired an accountant, simply enter *www.irs.gov*, click the tab "Apply for an Employer ID Number," and answer the questions. This is going to take you two days because the IRS has a policy of only issuing one EIN per applicant per day.

Even though you now have your EINs in hand, creating new accounts under the name of the Probate Estate or the Trust Estate is going to be a fair amount of work and it is essential that you develop a personal rapport with a banker—not the walk-up window teller, not the greeter who asks how they may help you today, but a person with a desk. Ideally, that should be the branch manager.

When my parents died in 2010, all of their bank accounts were with Bank of America. I had to open their Probate Estates in Montgomery County, Pennsylvania, because that was their county of residence. I, however, live in Virginia. So when I returned home and obtained EINs for their Probate Estates, I paid a visit to the largest branch of Bank of America in my neighborhood. There I asked to talk to the branch manager. And, even though my parents had all of their accounts with Bank of America, the fact that their probate cases were in Philadelphia made for some bureaucratic wrangling that required and hour and a half of phone calls between bank offices and a great deal of paper shuffling before they were finally able to establish the probate checking accounts. The moral of the story is this: Find the bank employee with the biggest office or you are going to be there all day.

Brokers

When laymen use the term, broker, they are usually referring to one of two things. Either they are referring to the individual who places orders to buy and sell stock for them, commonly referred to as a stock broker, or they are referring to the brokerage that is the company that employs the stock broker (e.g., Merrill Lynch). While your banker is helpful in the transition of accounts from decedent's name to entity name (i.e., Probate Estate or Trust Estate), the broker is going to keep you out of trouble.

Every executor and every trustee is known as a fiduciary—a title that comes with the highest level of legal obligation known to the law. You are absolutely, totally, 100% responsible for the preservation and investment of your estate. Mess up and violate your fiduciary duty—intentionally or not—you are looking at removal, lawsuits and, possibly, jail time. When cash, stocks, and bonds comprise a large portion of your estate, you have a duty to invest them as would "a prudent person." This Prudent Person Standard means you can be neither too conservative (e.g., converting the stocks and bonds into cash and hiding the money in a mattress) nor too aggressive (e.g., offshore drilling ventures). The balance falls in the middle, and a good broker will know the difference. Your job is to find a good broker.

Title Companies

Quick! How do you know that the home you are planning to sell hasn't already been sold to someone else? How can you be sure that it doesn't sit on land belonging to a Native American tribe? How can you be sure that it doesn't have a government easement the size of Montana running right down the middle of it? You know because of the tireless work of title companies. A title company's job is to ensure us that the property we are buying or selling does not in some way, great or small, belong to someone else. This, despite the fact that, in the vast majority of cases, the home and the land it is sitting on does not belong to anyone other than the guy who is selling it. Still, title companies look for interests that other people may have such as a disputed border with a neighbor or perhaps oil under your land that has been leased to an oil company. These interests become what is known as "clouds on the title." Potentially, they can cause you grave problems if you proceed to settlement being completely unaware of the cloud. And the bank giving you the mortgage to buy the house is keenly aware of it; okay, actually, it is their lawyers who are keenly aware of it. Nevertheless, however overblown the danger may be, a bank will insist on the services of the title company as a condition of providing the mortgage money. For you, the executor or trustee trying to sell the house, this will mean extra costs for either you or your buyer. And it will almost always mean delays.

Essentially, title are comprised of three kinds of employees: the title searcher, the attorney, and the settlement agent. The title searcher examines the history of ownership using the county's Office of Land Records. If an Indian burial ground is revealed, it will appear in the title examination. The lawyer reviews the deeds, forming what is called the "chain of title" (usually over the past 60 years) and looks for flaws in those documents. Of course, nobody is perfect and either the title searcher or the lawyer may make a mistake so, in an over-abundance of caution, your buyer will be offered a Title Insurance Policy; and the bank will insist on its purchase. And, finally, when every obsessive-compulsive impulse and fear has been assuaged, the settlement agent will oversee the signing of the deed, the mortgage, and all the related documents. As the Brits would say, "It's all stuff and nonsense," but it is the accepted procedure nevertheless. So you are just going to have to grin and bear it.

Perhaps you have bought and sold a home or two in your lifetime and were completely oblivious to the fact that a title company had even been involved. So, reading this, you are thinking "Why is this guy going on such a rant about it?" Ah, the difference my newly minted executor/trustee is that you never sold a home as a fiduciary before. The power of individuals to sell a home is fairly well established and respected, even among title companies. But they don't see nearly as many sales by fiduciaries and that makes all the difference.

Let me tell you a cautionary tale. At the beginning of my career, the statutes in my state made it very clear that a trustee had the power to sell real estate held in the name of the trust. To ensure that title companies knew this, I referenced the statute in the trust document. But that was not good enough. They did not want to have to read the statute; I had to state, unambiguously in the trust document, that the trustee had the power to sell trust real estate. But after a time, that was not enough either. I was told that the deed that conveyed the real estate to the trust must also contain a statement that the trustee had the power to sell that real estate at a later time. Being young and naïve, I protested that the deed did not establish the trustee's powers. It was the trust document that did that. I said, "The deed can say that the trustee is the queen of England; that doesn't make it so." But they insisted and I relented. After that, came the insistence that we amend the trust document to contain language that the title company's attorney liked better than mine. After that, I was told that I had to vow that the trustee had the power to sell trust real estate in something they called an "opinion letter." And, most recently, I am asked to simply remove the property from the trust before it is even listed for sale. In short, title companies are the poster child for obsessive-compulsive disorder. But that's who they are, and there is absolutely nothing you can do about it. If a title issue comes up the day before closing, let your attorney deal with it. Just know that closing is never tomorrow.

Summing Up

Up until this chapter, the theme of this book has been teamwork. You select the people who can do the work of settling your decedent's estates and you just oversee the process. But I would be remiss had I not explained that there are people involved in this process that you did not, and probably would not, hire. Bureaucrats, both government and private, make their living serving an overly complex, arbitrary, inefficient, rule-driven, paper-driven industry. If there is an exception to this rule, it would be the bankers and brokers. In every other instance, you must accept that dealing with a bureaucrat will rarely go smoothly. Let your team handle those issues and, just remember, be nice.

Things to Do

1. If you haven't already done so, provide the members of your team with the information necessary to complete the relevant paperwork (e.g., tax statements, deeds, insurance claim forms).
2. Follow up to ensure that all bureaucratic paperwork has been filed and received, and that the requested actions have been taken.
3. Be nice.

Chapter 9

The Banker: Keeper of the Cash

As you may recall from Chapter 8, "Know Your Bureaucrat," a banker can be either a valuable member of your team or simply an unreliable cog in a bureaucratic machine. Although it is tempting to call the 800 number on your decedent's last bank statement, you are far more likely to get professional and effective help from a real person you can talk to, face to face. So, as I emphasized in that chapter, go to the decedent's bank and ask to speak to the branch manager. Chat a bit. Get to know each other. If the branch manager seems competent, lay out your problems, questions, and concerns.

If the manager seems utterly clueless and is struggling to hide that fact, it will become apparent no more than 10 minutes into the conversation. If that is the case, you may want to simply state that you are the executor for the estate of one of their customers and you were wondering what you should do next. You don't have to take notes at this point, or even listen to the answer. You've determined that working with this particular bank employee will be counter-productive and you're just being polite. Then go to another branch, and another after that, until you find someone who is familiar with Probate Estates and makes you feel confident that they can be genuinely helpful. If necessary, go to another bank altogether; funds can always be moved from one bank to another bank.

I don't mean to be judgmental or condescending but logic dictates that the branch manager is likely to have had far more experience dealing with living customers as opposed to dead ones. Even so, there are many who have seen it all and done it all. This is the person you truly need.

The Estate Checking Account

At a very minimum, the Probate Estate is going to need a checking account to pay for Probate

Estate expenses such as court costs, legal fees, and accounting fees. To open a checking account for the Probate Estate, you are going to need an Employer Identification Number (EIN), your decedent's death certificate, and a small amount of cash (less than $100). If necessary, use your own cash and reimburse yourself later (see Chapter 12). If your banker has done this before, it will be a small matter to set up the account. Once established, you will deposit into that account all of the following:

1. Checks made out to your decedent;
2. Checks made out to your decedent's estate;
3. Proceeds from the sale of Probate Assets (e.g., real estate, jewelry, securities);
4. Cash that was in your decedent's possession on the date of death (e.g., in a safe or safe deposit box); and most important
5. Cash contained in any bank accounts that were in the decedent's name alone. Those accounts must now be closed.

If the will directs the probate assets to a living trust, you will do that later. This is where you start.

Other Kinds of Bank Accounts

In a nutshell, bank accounts all share two traits: interest rate and availability. As a rule, the higher the interest rate, the more restricted the availability. In other words, if you need to access the money on a routine basis, it's going to cost you. There are essentially four kinds of bank accounts: Checking, Savings, Money Market, and Certificates of Deposit. (In the case of credit unions, there is also something called a Share Account. A Share Account, however, is a minimal account you keep open just so that you can avail yourself of credit union benefits such as low-interest car loans.)

At one time, Checking accounts paid interest on money left in the account. That is not the case anymore. Oh, you may be able to find a Checking account that pays interest but it is, more often than not, just a Money Market account with check-writing privileges. If you write too many checks, the interest disappears; or they may simply convert it to a Checking account.

Savings accounts pay a little more interest (anything is more than nothing). But, again, although you may draw money out of a Savings account, it is supposed to be an occasional thing—if ever at all.

Money Market accounts pay still more interest (though often less than 1% per year). In most cases, Money Market accounts are indistinguishable from Savings accounts. Your money is available to you but the interest rate will decline if you use it like a checking account.

Certificates of Deposit (CDs) are where the action is when it comes to interest rates. Although once considered ridiculously low, a CD that pays 5% is considered to be outrageous nowadays and a find equivalent to striking oil. You are more likely to find these CD rates at small banks. Small banks tend to offer a better rate than the big boys since they don't have the name recognition to attract new customers. But as I said, the higher the interest rate, the less the availability. In fact, you can't draw money out of a CD at all. You have the option to close out the CD but, if you do, you will usually forfeit at least the last quarter's accrued interest.

What you should take away from this is that, as an executor, you really only need two kinds of bank accounts: Checking and CDs. Savings and Money Market accounts simply pay too little interest to justify parking any of the estate's cash there. Since you have a fiduciary obligation to put the estate assets to work, any cash that you don't expect to need for administering the estate can be invested in CDs. Cash you need to operate the estate should be in checking.

It should be noted that the line between brokerage houses and banks is gradually blurring. Most large banks now have a securities division. So, instead of calling your stock broker to invest estate money, you can just as easily invest that money with your banker. In some cases, such as Bank of America, the bank actually owns the brokerage (i.e., Merrill Lynch). However, each bank has its own procedures and structure. For example, although Bank of America has its own securities division, my understanding is that it is meant for small investors. A wealthier investor, or a large estate, will probably be more comfortable working with a Merrill Lynch–type brokerage.

The Trust Accounts

Your decedent may also have had trust accounts with the bank. It is far easier for most bankers to deal with trust accounts after a death than to establish a new Probate Estate account. All they need is the trust's new EIN. Up until your decedent's date of death, the decedent's revocable trust tax number was his Social Security number. Now your accountant simply needs to apply for a new EIN. If you don't have an accountant, just as you did for the Probate Estate, go to www .irs.org and follow the instructions.

This is an important step that many trustees miss. The bank reports interest paid to the trust using whatever tax number they have available. If all they have is the decedent's Social Security number, that is how they will report interest to the IRS. When you file the decedent's final tax return, IRS computers will be looking for the interest that now belongs to the trust. At the very least, this will require that the bank issue a revised report to the IRS; and often, the bank is unwilling to do that. The worst-case scenario could be an audit. And that is something that you really do not need.

FDIC

Since you are a fiduciary, and as I have said, you are held to the highest standard of care, you should never have an estate or trust bank account that is not properly insured. The Federal Deposit Insurance Corporation is an independent agency of the federal government. It is charged with insuring bank customer deposits against loss (e.g., the result of a run on the bank or bank failure). They guarantee the safety of trust and estate accounts up to $250,000 per beneficiary of the trust or the estate. So, for example, let's say that your decedent's Probate Estate and your decedent's Trust Estate both have accounts with Bank of America. The will names the trust as its only beneficiary (one beneficiary) and the trust names four beneficiaries. The sum of the Probate Estate accounts are insured up to $250,000. However, the sum of the trust accounts is insured up to $250,000 *per beneficiary* or $1,000,000. You must always be aware of these limits. Although it is rare for a bank to fail these day, it's your skin if your bank does fail and any part of the accounts are uninsured.

Claiming Accounts of the Contract Estate

Remember, the Contract Estate consists, in part, of bank accounts that are either in joint name with a living person or bank accounts that are in your decedent's name alone but payable on death (POD) to a living beneficiary. Strictly speaking, it is not your job to assist in the claim of these accounts but, since you need their values for purposes of filing the Federal Estate Tax Return, it would be helpful to both you and the claimant to lend assistance. Remember, however, that it is the accounts' co-owner or beneficiary who is actually making the claim. Unless you are an attorney, every phase of the claim must be by them. So if you need to follow up on the claim, you will probably need to bring the respective party with you when you visit the bank.

In an ideal world, all the bank needs is an original death certificate for the joint owner or the beneficiary (POD) to claim the account in their own name. But this is not an ideal world. Remember, banks are, by their very nature, bureaucracies. You should begin the process by contacting your banker (the one with whom you have established a relationship) and asking what is required for a co-owner or beneficiary to claim the account. (Almost always, there will at least be a claim form to fill out in addition to the death certificate.) Your banker will send these documents (usually by internal courier) to the proper department for processing. And then you wait.

Recently, I represented a young man who was the beneficiary of this father's checking account. It was not a huge sum—something like $6,000. Since it was such a small amount, I called the bank's Estate Division and asked for their claim procedure. They e-mailed a claim

form to me and instructed me to fax both the completed claim form and the death certificate to a specific
fax number. So I did. Two weeks went by and my young
client had not received his money. So I dropped by one
of the bank's branches and asked a man with a desk
to help me. He contacted the Estate Division and was
told that they had no record of the claim. (He rolled
his eyes and whispered to me, "Sometimes they shred
them.") Fortunately, I had the original paperwork I had
faxed and so the banker scanned it and sent it to them
electronically. Four weeks pass and still my young client does not have his check. I located a different banker
in the same branch and told him my tale of woe. He
submitted the claim for a third time. Four weeks later,
my young client finally had his money. Sometimes, the
bureaucracy cannot be avoided. Your only option is
persistence—making use of your banker to assist you.

Safe Deposit Boxes

It is exceedingly rare for someone to put his safe deposit
box in a trust name. It is only slightly less unusual for
someone to hold a safe deposit box in joint name. More
often than not, the box (which the bank treats just like
any other account) is in your decedent's name alone.

So, technically, the contents of the box are part of the Probate Estate. So, you would think that all you would need to do to empty the box is to locate the appropriate bank branch and present your Probate Certificate. Thereafter, you would move the contents of the box to a new safe deposit box under the Probate Estate's name. And, in an ideal world, that is really all you should have to do. But, like I said, no ideal world here or anywhere to be found.

For example, my parents were residents of Pennsylvania and Pennsylvania has an inheritance tax. When my father passed away, I called the small bank that housed his safe deposit box. I explained to them that I was the executor and that I would like to claim the contents of the box. I was told that, in the Commonwealth of Pennsylvania, I first had to send a letter, by certified mail, to the treasurer of Pennsylvania, located in the capital of Harrisburg, which was more than a hundred miles away. In that letter, I had to inform the treasurer that I would be appearing at that particular bank, on a particular date, at a particular time, to empty the box, just in case they wanted to send a state representative to inventory the contents. I was then to bring a certified copy of the letter to the bank, on the particular date, at the particular time, and present it to a banker there.

When the hour arrived, then and only then, would I be permitted to view and remove the contents of the safe deposit box. No representative ever appeared and the box was empty. This is why lawyers charge by the hour.

On the brighter side. The branch manager, seeing my frustration, took pity on me and waived the $75 rental fee for that year. There was not much else she could have done, but it was a nice gesture nevertheless.

Summing Up

If the decedent had bank accounts, you will need to determine if they are:

1. In trust name,
2. In joint name,
3. In the decedent's name alone but names a beneficiary (POD), or
4. In the decedent's name alone but with no named beneficiary.

You will need to provide the bank with the new trust EIN for No. 1, assist in making the claim for No. 2 and No. 3, and take possession of No. 4 and deposit the proceeds into a new Probate Estate checking account. Being mindful of the FDIC insurance limits, you will then move any cash you won't be needing from the Probate Estate checking account to a high-yield (admittedly a relative term) Certificate of Deposit. Assuming that your decedent had a safe deposit bank, you will need to take possession of the contents, open a safe deposit box in the name of the Probate Estate, and transfer the contents to the new box—where you will hold them until you decide whether to distribute them, sell them, or trash them.

Things to Do

1. If you have not already done so, open a checking account for the Probate Estate.
2. Be sure that any existing trust accounts have the trust's new EIN.
3. Deposit all of the following into the Probate checking account: cash, checks made payable to the decedent, and checks made payable to the decedent's Probate Estate.
4. Use high-yield CDs as needed.
5. Open a safe deposit box for the Probate Estate to secure jewelry, coins, precious metals, and anything else of value.

Chapter 10

The Realtor:
The Miracle Worker

Almost all of the members of your team perform critical tasks to keep you on track and out of trouble. But a good realtor is essential. While you might be able to muddle through without your accountant or even without your attorney, trying to sell your decedent's real estate on your own gives a whole new meaning to the word "foolish." As probably one of the single most valuable assets your decedent owned, you must handle it with care. Sell it for less than it is worth and your beneficiaries will not be happy with you— sometimes unhappy enough to attempt your removal, perhaps unhappy enough to sue you.

However, before we delve into the importance of your realtor, it is important to first mention that you may not even have the authority to sell the real estate. In some states, real estate may pass directly to the decedent's heirs (i.e., next of kin) at the moment of death. It is often pointed out that we don't have this result provided the real estate was in trust, had a joint owner, or was specifically given to someone in the will. Nevertheless, the importance of this quirk in the law should never be underestimated. For example, let's say that your decedent had a living trust but had no known will. Let's also say that the decedent was a widower with seven children. In some states, the real estate would then be completely out of the executor's control. Title would be vested in the seven children. As a result, all of the children would have to be involved in the sale (i.e., signing listing agreements, contracts, deeds, and being present at closing). To make matters worse, some title companies, not being certain whether the executor has an interest in the property or not but keen on protecting themselves, would require that all seven children *and* the executor be involved in the sale. And what if one of the children is a minor? In that case, the court would need to appoint a legal representative for the child (often referred to as a guardian ad litem) and the title company would then require the six adult children and the executor and the guardian ad litem to be involved in the sale. Given half a minute, I can conjure up a dozen more unexpected and infuriating results because of this law but you get the point. Before you list the property for sale, call your lawyer and make certain that you, the executor, have sole power to list it and sell it.

Comfortable with your authority to sell the real estate, your next job is clear. You must find and hire a good realtor. You can use a referral service like Angie's List, but I strongly recommend a referral from someone you know and trust; someone who has used the realtor themselves. When my parents passed away, I found myself without a realtor I could trust since my parents resided in Pennsylvania and I was a Virginian. But I remembered that my in-laws were also from Pennsylvania and were pleased with the realtor they used. That realtor turned out to be more competent and professional than I could have hoped. She suffered with me through the endless problems associated with homes that appear to have been all but abandoned. But through shear patience and determination, she got the properties sold.

The Process

Once you have selected a real estate agent, the agent will take over for you but, in a nutshell, there are five steps in the process of selling real estate: Assessment, Listing, Negotiation, Contract, and Closing. And the Negotiation and Contract steps may have to be repeated more than once. In fact, my Pennsylvania real estate agent and I went through about a dozen rounds of negotiation and contracts with about a dozen different buyers. How does someone sign a contract and then get out of it? Let me count the ways. But more about that later in this chapter.

When you have found an agent, the first thing you will need to do is sign a Listing Agreement. The Listing Agreement usually gives the agent and the agency the exclusive right to sell a specific property for you. A description of the property, usually adorned with flattering photos and a colorful, if somewhat exaggerated, description of its many fine features, then goes onto a national database (known as the Multiple Listing Service) for other real estate agents to review. The hope is that an agent who represents a prospective buyer will take note of your property and make an appointment with your agent to view the home. In addition, your agent will probably publish a similar advertisement in the real estate section of local newspapers, conduct an "open house" for potential buyers who don't have an agent, and employ a myriad of other advertising techniques to get your property seen.

Prior to actually posting your property on the Multiple Listing Service, your agent will probably want to assess its condition. The agent knows what damage is cosmetic and what damage is a deal breaker. In one of my parent's homes, it was hard to miss a gaping hole in the ceiling. Looking up at it, I said, "Maybe we could just sell it as is." Her response was, "yeah . . . no." I was instructed as to precisely what required fixing and what could be overlooked. And the work had to be completed before she would even consider showing the property to anyone.

Once the repairs are complete and the house is on the Multiple Listing Service, your agent will begin fielding the offers. The offers will be forwarded to you for acceptance or rejection, but a good agent will advise you as to whether the offer is reasonable or just "low-balling" (i.e., an unreasonably low offer made in an attempt to convince you that your asking price is way too high). In addition to "low-balling," buyers and their agent may ask for any number of concessions, ranging from including the appliances to paying the closing costs. Your agent will advise you accordingly. This is the Negotiation phase of the sale.

Negotiation is more art than science. That is to say, you and your agent need to be creative. First of all, the agent will attempt to create an emotional response in the prospective buyers. Although it may seem silly to a hardened business person, making sure that the lawn is cut and trimmed, that the bushes are neatly manicured, and that years of overgrowth have been removed creates what real estate agents call "curb appeal." In other words, the sale begins from the moment the home comes into view. It is true that some people can look at what amounts to a shed and see a palace. However, most people will just see the shed.

Inside the house, it is not enough that repairs have been made. Real estate agents use a tactic called "staging." The home becomes a set on a stage. There is furniture. Flowers in the foyer. A bowl of fruit in the kitchen. Sometimes, there is even the aroma of freshly baked cookies. In short, prospective buyers are made to see a home and not a hovel. Again, creating a positive emotional response is critical and a good real estate agent will be a master of it.

Beyond making your decedent's property appealing at a visceral level, there are some additional tried and true negotiation tactics you need to consider. First, never low-ball the property. You may believe in your heart that the house isn't worth a quarter and two box tops but you cannot let a prospective buyer know that. Instead, go to a free appraisal site such as Zillow.com and see what they think your property is worth. Such websites base their appraisal on what homes of similar size, age, and amenities have been selling for in your neighborhood. Of course, you could use an actual appraiser but that is going to cost you at least $500. On the other hand, as I mentioned in Chapter 6, the IRS prefers a valuation by a licensed appraiser.

Second, do not take the first offer. Wait and see what else comes through the door. You and your agent may have a pretty good idea of what the property is worth, but some offers may surprise you. In fact, if you get at least two offers, your agent may be able to prompt a bidding war. It is human nature to want something just because somebody else wants it (a phenomenon that has kept the art industry in business for centuries). Just mentioning that another prospective buyer has offered more will usually net you a better offer.

On the other hand, you may be sitting on a property that seems better suited for the slums of Mumbai and no amount of curb appeal or staging is going to change that. At best, it's a fixer-upper and so it has to be sold that way. In such cases, you can sell the house "as is." What you get in such cases is far, far below what Zillow just told you the house should be worth. But sometimes you have no choice. Just a heads up: Not everyone understands the concept of "as is." When I discovered that additional repairs to my parents' house were going to cost more than the value they would add, my agent offered the house for sale "as is." One young couple said that they would buy the house "as is" if I fixed it up first.

Once a deal has been stuck, your agent will reduce it to a contract that both you and the buyer will sign. It is imperative that you review the contract carefully. If you don't feel up to the task, ask your lawyer to review it to ensure: (1) that the contract correctly and thoroughly reflects the deal that was struck, and (2) that there are no unreasonable escape clauses. There is usually one or more reasonable escape clauses for the buyer. The most common of these is a clause that makes the sale contingent on the buyer obtaining financing (i.e., getting a mortgage). Another common escape hatch is making the sale contingent on the approval of the buyer's home inspector. Again, not an unreasonable request. In the case of my parent's residence, it was the home inspector clause that allowed at least five prospective buyers to tear up the contract. As it turns out, despite six months of repairs, nobody noticed the mold growing in a crawl space. Rather than further costly delays, and with the agreement of my agent, I sold the house in "as is" condition for $50,000 less than our original asking price. Apparently, a hole in the ceiling is always a deal breaker; mold, not necessarily.

After the contract has been reviewed and signed by both you and the buyer, you proceed to closing. In times past, both parties and their lawyers would show up at a designated location (usually the title company) to sign all of the documents related to the sale, such as the deed, the mortgage, and the promissory note, as well as a plethora of disclosure documents intended to prevent the seller from making false claims and, essentially, pulling a "fast one" on the buyer. These days, however, it is more common to give your agent a limited power of attorney to attend closing in your place, especially if you live 200 miles away like I did. Yet one more service that your agent provides.

Your Contractor

If you are really, really lucky, your decedent's home will be immaculate and in spectacular condition. If not, you will probably want to bring in a contractor for repairs before your agent shows the house to a single prospective buyer.

Finding a good contractor is not quite as easy as finding a good real estate agent. Mention that you have a house in need of repairs to any friend or acquaintance and you will quickly be handed phone number for brothers, boyfriends, in-laws, cousins, neighbors, and/or all of their respective spouses. Unless, you have first-hand knowledge of the person's work, you should just smile, say "thank you," and then, as soon as you're alone, throw the numbers away—mainly because you don't know the motivation for the referral. You just might be having this contractor thrust upon you because he hasn't worked in six months and not because he does great work. Instead, go to a review website such as Angie's List. I have used such websites on numerous occasions and rarely have I been disappointed.

Once you have found a contractor, ask for an estimate (i.e., a detailed projection of what each repair will cost) and then discuss the terms of payment. Most real estate repair work is paid in increments that are tied to the progress that has been made. For example, when the floor has been refinished, the contractor is paid for the cost of refinishing the floor as set forth in the estimate. When the hole in the ceiling has been repaired, the contractor is paid for that part of the overall estimate, and so forth and so on. Most contractors have their own contracts that explain these incremental payments. If not, ask your lawyer to draft one for you.

The contract should also spell out the time needed to complete each repair and should include the phrase, "Time is of the essence." "Time is of the essence" is *your* escape clause if the work is dragging on past the promised completion dates. Your job is to administer the estate in a timely manner and that includes liquidating assets such as homes as quickly as possible.

It is also important that your contractor be bonded and insured. Bonded means that you are protected if the contractor doesn't do his job. In other words, if the contractor doesn't complete the job, does a poor job, doesn't pay his subcontractors, or fails to get the necessary permits, it's not your problem and you are made whole. Insured is similar to your homeowner's insurance. If the contractor burns down your house, you're covered.

Once the work is underway, you need to monitor the contractor's progress. This can be time-consuming and frustrating but it needs to be done. When my parents passed away, and I was faced with massive repairs to their homes, I hired a contractor in Philadelphia on the strength of a friend's referral. He was skilled and did great work but neither my friend nor the contractor happened to mention that he was also a full-time high school teacher. Jobs that should have taken weeks stretched into months. Since I live in Virginia and the homes were in Pennsylvania, I was forced to use my weekends to drive to Philadelphia (3 ½ hours each way) and check on the progress. Had I not been there to oversee and nag, I am fairly certain that the repairs would still be a work in progress to this day, five years later.

However, there is an alternative to contractors. If you are a very fortunate executor, your decedent's home will be located in a desirable neighborhood— one where the value of the lot far exceeds that of a 1950's era, one-level, barracks-style, post-war, wreck of a rambler starter home that has suffered from substandard construction these past six decades. These are known as "tear-downs." And your real estate agent advertises it as such. In the Washington, D.C., suburb of Vienna, Virginia, it seems like almost every home sold is a tear-down. Houses that are so old and in such disrepair that they make a mobile home look like a Malibu beach house are routinely sold for top dollar and then razed to the ground. What replaces them are mini-mansions that come within inches of the property line on all sides. But, like I said, a very desirable neighborhood. So, if you find yourself with a "tear-down," consider yourself blessed.

Summing Up

A good real estate agent is an enormous asset. But before your agent can help you liquidate the property, check with your lawyer to ensure that you, as executor, have the sole power to sell it. After that, have your agent assess the condition of the property. If repairs are needed, use an independent referral site to find a good contractor. Once repairs are completed, your agent will list the property and begin fielding offers. Always negotiate from a position of strength and give the impression that your decedent's real estate is a genuine find for anyone looking to buy. Once you have an offer, have your lawyer review the contract for unreasonable escape clauses and, if the contract is reasonable, sign it. Then proceed to closing.

Things to Do

1. Consult your lawyer to assess your authority to sell.
2. Interview and select your realtor.
3. Select a good contractor as needed.
4. Have your appraiser value the repaired property.
5. Have your lawyer review the sales contract.

Chapter 11

The Broker: Meeting Your Fiduciary Obligations

Buying and selling securities is probably the one financial activity that most Americans know nothing about. Even though about half of Americans participate in a 401(k) or similar retirement plan through work, the vast majority leave the investment decisions to the plan administrator who, in turn, usually relies upon the advice of a broker. So, it seems prudent to begin this chapter with an explanation of the terminology used by an industry that both reflects and affects the world's economy.

Broker and Brokerage

Collectively, investments such as stocks and bonds are known as securities. The people who invest in securities usually do so through a regulated professional known as a broker (aka a stockbroker). The broker, in turn, usually works for a brokerage (aka a brokerage house). This can get confusing when investors, the media, and sometimes brokers themselves also refer to the brokerage as a "broker." The easiest way to remember the difference is that the shorter term, broker, refers to a person. But the longer term, brokerage, refers to the company that employs many brokers. So, for example, my friend, Lindsay Veleber, is a broker who works for the brokerage Edward Jones.

Securities

There are many kinds of securities, but if the decedent owned any it was probably stocks or bonds. Stocks are simply shares of ownership in a corporation. So, for example, if the corporation has issued a thousand shares of stock, and you own 500 of those shares, you own 50% of the company. And since stockholders are the owners of the company, the corporation's directors may pay the stockholders a portion of the corporate profit, known as dividends. Though the corporation may provide proof of your ownership by giving you a stock certificate, that practice has been all but abandoned.

Rather, these days, your investment appears only in the records of the corporation and your brokerage.

Bonds are debt investments. In other words, you are lending money to either a corporation or a government (federal, state, or local). In return, the entity borrowing the money pays you interest, usually every three months. United States Savings Bonds are the best known of these investments. You may also come across something known as a municipal bond. Municipal bonds are issued by a local government and are popular because the interest they pay is usually tax-free.

There are other investments that appear to be securities but are actually vehicles for buying, selling, or holding securities for the investor. The most common of these are mutual funds. A share of a mutual fund represents ownership in a collection of stock chosen and managed by the fund manager. Finally, there are retirement vehicles such as IRAs, 401(k)s, and annuities—all of which can hold stocks, bonds, and mutual funds. IRAs frequently own annuities as well. All of this can get very confusing. Just remember that at the heart of almost all investments are either stock (ownership investments) or bonds (debt investments).

If your decedent used a broker then you, as the executor or trustee, will receive monthly or quarterly statements from the brokerage detailing the account's investments. At first, these statements appear to lack anything resembling a logical structure. However, with a little effort, you will soon be able to make sense of them. (If not, the broker is always there to help you out.) Regardless of the brokerage, the statements always contain a summary page that sets forth the total value of each type of investment, followed by several pages that set forth the particulars of each investment (e.g., number of shares of each stock owned). Some brokerages provide separate statements for IRAs, but not necessarily. If you are reading a combined statement, the IRA will have its own account number.

In reviewing the statement, you may notice a cash or money market component of the account. For the most part, the cash came from stock dividends or bond interest payments. This is ready cash that is available to you for paying the decedent's bills. It is accessible immediately just as if it were a checking account. Furthermore, while the cash is going to essentially remain unchanged, a stock that has been steadily growing in value or paying dividends will usually continue to do so. Since it is part of your fiduciary duty to maximize the value of an estate's assets, it is preferable to use available cash before liquidating (i.e., selling) a productive stock. In other words, if you callously kill the goose that's laying the golden eggs, you may get yourself in trouble with your beneficiaries.

Of course, you don't have to wait for a statement to review your decedent's investments. All major brokerages now give their investors access to their accounts online. As the executor or trustee, you just need to register on the brokerage's website. Most even provide a smartphone-friendly version of the site so you can check up on your estate's investments from anywhere, any time of day. If it becomes necessary to sell any of the securities, or even buy more, that can usually be done from your phone as well. And if your brokerage is owned by your bank (e.g., Merrill Lynch and Bank of America), you can even move the cash component to a bank checking account faster than you can say, "Online Banking."

Non-Brokered Securities

It is possible, though not likely, that some of your decedent's investments are in certificate form. That is to say, there may be physical stock certificates. You may not even know they exist until a statement or dividend check arrives from the corporation. If such is the case, you are going to have to locate them. Check the obvious places such as safes and safe deposit boxes. However, I have had some clients who simply left them in a desk drawer, along with their deed, will, and other valuable papers. If all else fails, carefully sift through the pile of mail on the dining room and kitchen tables.

Once the certificate has been located, turn it over to your broker. If your decedent did not have a broker, this is the time to hire one. In fact, all non-brokerage securities should be turned over to a broker who will then do the work of incorporating them into a broker-age account. As you are about to see, you don't need to have a lot of experience with securities so long as you have a broker.

Your Broker's Role

For the most part, a broker's job is to provide investment advice and take trade orders (i.e., customer requests to buy and sell securities). But for our purposes, your broker will provide three additional critical services: accepting non-brokered securities, consolidating invest-ment accounts, and creating beneficiary accounts.

As we discussed above, not all securities are held by a brokerage. So, once you have selected a brokerage, your first order of business is to provide the broker with any and all non-brokered securities. Your broker will advise you as to whether you should add these investments to your new account or sell them. You will probably be advised to keep investments in the more solid companies (often called Blue Chip Stocks), such as Disney, and sell those companies that are on their way down. In fact, don't be surprised if the decedent owned stock in companies that no longer exist. Many senior citizens go for decades without reviewing their portfolios.

You may also find that your decedent worked with many different brokers, mutual fund managers, and retirement account administrators. It is important that all of these accounts be consolidated with your new brokerage. Your job is going to be hard enough without having to track a dozen different investment accounts and interpret their wildly diverse monthly or quarterly statements. Unless you just enjoy working needlessly, it is best to consolidate and simplify.

Finally, when you are ready to begin making distributions, you may distribute the securities by simply having your broker establish a new account for each beneficiary. For example, let's say that at the time of distribution, your Probate Estate or Trust

Estate brokerage account is worth $1 million in stocks and bonds. Let us also say that the beneficiaries are five adult children. Your broker would simply create five new accounts (one for each child) and transfer $200,000 worth of stocks and bonds from the estate's brokerage account into each of the new beneficiary accounts.

Now be careful here. It is not enough to simply transfer securities that are worth $200,000 at the time of distribution because, by the close of business the next day, those values will have changed. If one child got stock that went down while another child got stock that went up, you are going to have at least one very unhappy beneficiary. No, what you must ask your broker to do is to transfer into each beneficiary's account securities that are not only equal in value but are absolutely identical. So, if John gets 40 shares of IBM, every one of his four siblings gets 40 shares of IBM. If John gets 50 shares of Microsoft, every child gets 50 shares of Microsoft. And so forth. To be perfectly honest, you will rarely achieve identical accounts. You may have to sell a little of the stock to get it right. Even then, someone usually winds up giving up a few pennies. If you are one of the beneficiaries, that someone should be you.

Your Role

You have a fiduciary duty to shepherd and maximize an estate's assets. Your broker can give you advice, but ultimately the burden rests on you. You may not be Warren Buffett, but there are a few rules of thumb that will keep you out of trouble.

1. Don't sell anything unless you absolutely need the cash to pay bills or if the stock is dropping faster than the Times Square ball on New Year's Eve—and even then, only with your broker's approval;
2. Don't buy anything (even if your broker thinks it's a good idea);
3. Allow the cash from interest and dividends to accumulate;
4. Review each brokerage statement as soon as you get it; and
5. Never hesitate to seek your broker's help or advice.

Of course these rules are not to be taken as absolute and inviolate. Every rule has its exceptions. You will know it when you see it. Just keep these rules in the back of your mind and review them before taking action.

Other Methods of Distribution

In addition to creating beneficiary accounts and filling them with identical securities, there are two other methods of distribution. They are distribution through liquidation and non-uniform distributions.

Distribution through liquidation is a simple concept. Let's return to my example of the five adult children and the million-dollar estate account. You simply call your broker and say, "sell everything." The proceeds of sale, less the broker's commission, is deposited into the cash portion of the brokerage account. Then you divide the cash account by five and write a check to each child for that amount. So, if the broker's commission was 5%, or $50,000, you would write a check to each child for $190,000.

That being said, I suggest that distribution through liquidation be used as a last resort. It is usually necessary when there is endless squabbling among the beneficiaries as to who gets what. In such instances you can use it as a threat. "Stop this fighting or I will simply turn everything into cash." It's the executor's way of saying, "Don't make me turn this car around."

The reason distribution through liquidation is not the best solution (as tempting as it may become) is that it carries costs. As I said, if the broker sells securities for you, the broker and the brokerage are entitled to compensation (i.e., the commission). In addition, and as we shall explore later in this chapter, there are usually tax consequences. Finally, it may result in one or more beneficiaries attempting to remove you or, worse, sue you for malfeasance. Nevertheless, you have a right to use liquidation if there appears to be no other way to close the estate.

Non-uniform distributions are distributions that are not identical in value or component securities. This seems to contradict what I said earlier and it does. What has happened in such cases is horse trading, plain and simple. Let's say, for example, that your decedent's estates consisted not only of securities but also real estate. Let's also say that one child insists on getting the real estate and is willing to forego a part if his securities for it. Finally, we will assume that the real estate is worth $175,000 (appraised value) and the securities are worth $825,000. Then in that case, four of the siblings take identical securities packages, each worth $200,000, and our problem child takes the real estate ($175,000) and the remaining securities ($25,000). The components of his securities package are identical to those of his siblings but proportionately smaller (e.g., each of his siblings got 40 shares of IBM but he gets only 5).

Despite all of the extra work you and your broker had to do just to make the problem child happy, it is still possible that he may later become dissatisfied with his choices and seek to alter the distribution yet again. To do that, he will point to the will or the trust and argue that the five children did not get equal shares as the will or trust required. To pre-empt this sort of nonsense, you employ a device known as a Beneficiaries Agreement, which can be drafted by your lawyer. In the Beneficiaries Agreement, all the beneficiaries agree that the distributions will not be identical and acknowledge that, because they are not identical shares, they may appreciate or depreciate differently. Your trouble maker is now stuck with his choice because you made the Beneficiaries Agreement a condition of the non-uniform distribution.

Taxes

Owning securities usually results in three different kinds of taxable income: interest, dividends, and capital gains (or losses). Interest and dividends will be reported to you in January on a form called a 1099.

Most brokerages show interest dividends and capital gains (or losses) on the same 1099. You will provide this form to your accountant to prepare your federal and state fiduciary tax returns. With a few exceptions, interest and dividends are taxed as ordinary income. That means that, if the 1099 says that your securities paid $100 worth of dividends, that is precisely what will show up on the fiduciary income tax return and precisely what will be passed through to the beneficiaries to report on their personal income tax returns. Capital gains and losses, however, are a different animal altogether. The 1099 does not usually reflect your sales activities so calculating capital gains and losses will be up to you. In addition, unlike interest and dividends, capital gains and losses are figures that you can manipulate.

Remember that the date of death value becomes the new cost basis. Proceeds minus basis equals capital gain or capital loss. If you have to liquidate securities to pay bills or to facilitate a distribution, you must consider what will generate the least capital gain. Ideally, you should sell something that will actually generate a capital loss. So, for example, if IBM was worth $50 per share on the date of death but now it is selling for $40 per share, selling 100 shares will yield a loss of $1,000 ([$40–$50] x 100).

In deciding what to sell, you have to look at the stock market as a whole. If IBM stock dropped $10 per share, as in my example, you have to ask if it was because the corporation was having difficulty or was it because the market as a whole was having difficulty. When stocks drop together, the event is called a "market correction." Market corrections really do not reflect the value of any individual company. Actually, what market corrections do reflect is the insecurity of investors on any given day. It was a market correction, after all, that gave us the Great Depression in 1929.

So, before selling IBM, make sure that other stocks have not dropped a proportionate amount. If you look at each stock, over the past three to five years, its upward or downward trend becomes evident (your brokerage will provide online charts). In this way, you can pick a true dog of an investment to unload. The effect is threefold. First, you have the cash you need. Second, the beneficiaries get a deduction. And, third, you have disposed of an investment that was pulling down the value of the estate, and in so doing, you have demonstrated that you understand your fiduciary duty.

Special Rules for IRAs

Although IRAs (i.e., Individual Retirement Accounts) most often hold securities, their tax treatment is governed by a different set of rules entirely. First and foremost, when your decedent makes someone the beneficiary of an IRA, the beneficiary gets what is called, not surprisingly, an Inherited IRA. While most retirement accounts require the owner to start withdrawing money from it by the time the owner reaches 70 ½ years of age, the recipient of an Inherited IRA must start drawing money out almost immediately (i.e., the Required Minimum Distribution or RMD). What difference does it make? Well, while the IRA is left alone, it grows, tax-free. But when you draw money out, the money you take is taxable as ordinary income. It doesn't matter that your broker had to sell stock that the IRA held in order to give you your RMD, the proceeds are not a capital gain. Nor are they a capital loss. The proceeds are treated just like interest and dividends.

One other interesting thing to note about Inherited IRAs: The Required Minimum Distribution is based on the beneficiary's age. All else being equal, the younger the beneficiary, the smaller the Required

Minimum Distribution. For example, a beneficiary who is 70 has a much larger RMD than the beneficiary who is 50. But the relationship between the disparate RMDs is not readily apparent. In fact, there are tables and formulas used to make the calculation. The good news is that every RMD will be calculated by the broker. (Incidentally, the tables and formulas used to make this calculation were so complicated that beneficiaries almost never got it right on their own. So the government simply enacted new regulations requiring the brokers to do it for them.)

Summing Up

Securities are, for the most part, stocks and bonds. Stocks represent ownership in a corporation and bonds represent a loan you have made to a corporation or government. Your broker works for a brokerage and has the primary function of providing investment advice as well as buying and selling securities for the customers. For you, the executor or trustee, the broker provides three additional and critical functions: transferring non-brokered assets into the estate's account, merging other brokered accounts into the estate's account, and setting up accounts for the beneficiaries to receive distributions. Although distributions are made to the beneficiaries in a uniform manner, they may take non-uniform distributions provided they all sign a Beneficiary Agreement. Securities produce three kinds of taxable income: interest, dividends, and capital gains and losses. You should always endeavor to maximize the estate and reduce taxes by selling securities that have been steadily declining in value and will produce the most deductible losses. Finally, remember that the tax rules governing Inherited IRAs differ from both the rules governing other types of IRAs as well as from the rules governing capital gains and losses.

Things to Do

1. Interview and select a broker.
2. Provide the broker with all of the decedent's most recent investment statements.
3. Provide the broker with the EINs for both the Probate Estate and the Trust Estate.
4. Provide the broker with all of the beneficiaries' personal information if beneficiary accounts are to be established.

Chapter 12

The Insurance Agent and the Life Insurance Lotto

The Concept

There was a time when life insurance was thought to be a solution looking for a problem. Even worse, the thought that someone would receive a lot of cash because a loved one had died seemed somehow unethical—and to some, even immoral. But times have changed and now everything is expensive, even death. The average cost of a funeral is over $10,000. The cost of settling your decedent's estate, including out-of-pocket expenses, court costs, professional fees, and your commission can consume up to 6% of total assets. Final medical bills that are not paid by health insurance can be enormous. And then you have the tax man, mortgage lenders, and noisy beneficiaries—all of whom cry that they need to be paid now. In short, the insurance solution has finally found its problem. And the problem is a need for immediate liquidity.

If you have never purchased life insurance or otherwise have no experience with it, rest assured that the concept is fairly simple. In fact, it's very much like the lottery. Like the lottery, you are betting that you will pick the winning number and collect the pot. With life insurance, the only difference is that the number you are picking is your date of death and the pot is called the death benefit. Put another way, the insurance company is betting that you will survive the term of the life insurance contract but you are betting that you won't. Because the insurance company has mathematicians called actuaries, they can calculate the odds of you dying during the term of the contract based on your age, weight, health, and habits. They then calculate how much you have to pay for the insurance in order to ensure that, in any given year, they will always make a profit. In other words, the house always wins.

For example, when I was 59 years old (last year), I agreed to pay my insurance company approximately $8,000 per year in exchange for a $1,400,000 death benefit. The term is 20 years. To ensure that I was not dying of anything neither of us knew about, they sent a nurse to my office to weigh me, take my blood pressure, wire me to an EKG machine, and draw blood. Turns out I am very healthy. If I survive the next 19 years, the insurance company comes out $160,000 ahead. If I die at some point in the next 19 years, my beneficiaries net a cool $1,400,000! But, from the insurance company's point of you, there are enough people like me who survive the term to offset the few who don't; and then some.

Types of Life Insurance

Level Term

Level Term life insurance is precisely what I purchased last year. I pay $8,000 per year (the premium) for 20 years (the term). If I die during that time, the insurance company pays my beneficiaries $1,400,000 (the death benefit, aka the face amount). At the end of the 20-year term, I have the option to continue the insurance contract for an astronomical premium (I will be 79, after all).

Whole Life Insurance

Whole Life insurance provides the insured with a cash reserve. A portion of each premium paid pays for the death benefit, just like Level Term life insurance. However, the remainder of the premium is invested with the insurance company. Over time, the invested portion (the cash value) grows. At any time, the insured can "cash in" the Whole Life policy, end the contract, and take the cash value. The annual premiums needed to purchase Whole Life insurance tend to be considerably higher than those needed to purchase Level Term.

Accidental Death

Contrary to what the media would have you believe, a surprisingly small percentage of deaths are the result of an accident. That is why there is a special type of life insurance that just covers accidental deaths. The death benefit can be very high even though the premium is relatively cheap. If life insurance were part of the gaming industry, accidental death would be right up there with Keno—cheap to play, big payout, but very poor odds of winning.

The Insurance Agent

As with securities, there are really two players in the insurance industry. There is the insurance agent and then there is the company who actually provides the insurance. The agent helps the consumer select a type of life insurance and, in return, the insurance company pays the agent a commission. Occasionally, you will come across an independent agent who can sell insurance policies from a myriad of insurance companies.

If your decedent owned life insurance, you may attempt to make a claim through the insurance company's 800 number, but I wouldn't recommend it. As with securities dealings, it is always preferable to work with an individual. More often than not, the agent will attempt to win future business from you by being as helpful as possible. For example, if you want to help a beneficiary file a claim with the insurance company, calling the 800 number will get you a blank form that you will need to fill out; sometimes the form comes with instructions and sometimes it does not. The agent, on the other hand, will provide the claim form, fill it out, and file it for you. After that, the agent will call to ensure that your beneficiary got the money. I would like to say that the two experiences are like night and day, but even that analogy doesn't begin to cover the gulf of professionalism that yawns between a disinterested and disembodied voice and a really good agent—an agent who gives you a home phone number and sends you birthday cards.

This is important because people often own multiple insurance policies with multiple companies. My father owned four policies that were with four different insurance companies. He named his five children as equal beneficiaries on each policy. Every insurance company told me that I and each of my siblings had to file our claims separately. The upshot was that, since I was chosen to settle all of the estates, including the Contract Estate, I had to complete 20 claim forms and then forward them to my siblings for signature. Had my father had a single insurance agent working for any one of the companies, my load would have been lightened immensely. Alas, that was not the case. Any agent my father had ever dealt with had died or retired.

It is important to note that many insurance companies require that each claim be submitted with an original death certificate. Death certificates cost about $15 each. Had my father's insurance companies required that each sibling send a death certificate with each claim form, it would have cost the estate an additional

$300. Fortunately for me, each company only asked for one death certificate; so we got off light, for only $60.

Forms of Payment

As a rule, an insurance company will offer you multiple claims options. Of course, most beneficiaries will request a check for the entire amount that is due to them, known as a lump sum. However, insurance companies offer at least three other options: a checking account, installment payments, or an annuity.

Most beneficiaries are surprised to learn that the insurance company will be happy to hold onto the death benefit and simply give the beneficiary a checkbook. The beneficiary can then write checks for whatever he needs or desires until the checking account is empty. Whether or not the account pays interest is up to the insurance company and the state insurance regulators.

The second option is installment payments. The insurance company pays the beneficiary a fixed amount on a regular basis (monthly, quarterly, annually, etc.). This method has the advantage of giving the beneficiary a fixed stream of income for a predetermined number of years.

The third option the insurance company may offer is to give the beneficiary payment in the form of an annuity. Like the installment method, the beneficiary gets a fixed payment each payment period. The difference is that the payments are for life. In other words, the payments don't end until the beneficiary does.

It is important to note that between the time that the insured dies and a lump sum payment is actually made, the insurance company has to pay interest on the unpaid death benefit. That is why you are rarely going to see a check that contains a round number; even if you are the only beneficiary. So, for example, if the death benefit was $100,000, the check that you receive will be more. If there is a lengthy delay (more than 60 days), state regulations may see to it that you receive a lot more.

Exclusions

In some case, the insurance company will not pay your beneficiaries. These are called exclusions and, quite frankly, they are common-sense escape clauses. Put simply, whenever the risk element has been removed, the insurance company is not required to pay. Just as a casino is not required to pay someone who has been cheating.

Suicide

In most states, an insurance company is not required to pay the death benefit if the insured committed suicide within one or two years after buying the policy. As an additional hedge against this risk, and especially in the cases of death benefits exceeding $1 million, many insurance companies will conduct a mental evaluation of the insurance applicant as well as the physical evaluation.

Murder

While homicide is not an excluded death per se, the insurance company will not pay someone who actually committed the murder. This is not so much insurance law as criminal law. Criminal law provides that a murderer may not benefit financially from his or her crime. This leaves open the question as to whether the insurance company will pay at all. In many cases, they will pay the estate of the victim and the estate will pay any beneficiary other than the murderer.

Fraud

When you fill out an insurance application, you answer a bushel basket of questions about your health, your health history, your family's health, and their health history. Lie about absolutely anything and the insurance company can claim fraud. So, if you know that your family has a history of congestive heart failure and you lie about that, your family won't be seeing any insurance proceeds when the big one gets you.

Failure to Pay

The Captain Obvious of the exclusions occurs when the insured has failed to pay the premiums. In most states (if not in all of them), an insurance company is required to give the insured notice that the life insurance policy is about to lapse unless an overdue premium is paid immediately. It doesn't matter that the beneficiary is not at fault or had no knowledge that the insured stop paying. A life insurance policy is a contract. Failure to pay the premiums is a breach of the contract. And the insurance company's recourse for the breach is to rescind the policy.

Uses for Life Insurance

The rule of thumb used to be that you need life insurance equal to five times your salary. I have no idea who came up with that rule or how they arrived at that amount, but it seems more than a little bit arbitrary. For executors, life insurance is simply an immediate source of cash. It spares you the dreaded decision of what to sell and what not to sell. With the exception of securities, executors almost always take a bath on the sale of estate assets. People seem to know that you are under pressure to sell and they will invariably take advantage of you. If your decedent had life insurance payable to the Probate Estate or to the Trust Estate, you don't need to get stressed or get taken.

This, of course, begs the question of who are the beneficiaries. If the beneficiary of your decedent's life insurance was not the Probate Estate or the Trust Estate, then the insurance will not be yours to use in any case. People are all too often comforted by the knowledge that they have life insurance to pay their bills when they die. But they don't think it through. If the kids are getting the proceeds, they are unlikely to surrender any money to the executor. So, the one obligated to pay the bills is, once again, forced to liquidate assets. If this is the case with your decedent, you may prevail upon the beneficiaries to release their rights to the insurance money. Most life insurance policies that have no beneficiary to pay will pay the Probate Estate by default. Your insurance agent will provide the form or format for the release. It may be a long shot, but it is certainly worth the effort.

Assuming your decedent made the life insurance payable to the estate, or made it payable to a beneficiary who has died, or made it payable to a living beneficiary who has released all right to it, take the proceeds as a lump sum. Then, if you have not already done so, open a checking account for the estate and deposit the life insurance proceeds. Finally, add whatever other cash you have to the account and prioritize your expenses in the following order:

1. Death Taxes: If your decedent's Federal Gross Estate (i.e., the sum of all four estates) has a value in excess of $5,450,000, ask you accountant to project the estate tax due. If your state has an estate tax or an inheritance tax, have your accountant project that as well. There are major civil and criminal penalties for failure to pay taxes.

Accordingly, death taxes, if any, will take priority when it comes to spending your available cash (including the life insurance proceeds). It is also possible that your decedent was liable for income tax as well for the period of January 1 up to and including the date of death. If the total projected tax liability exceeds the available cash, don't use them for anything else. Begin considering what estate assets you can sell. If your cash exceeds the total projected tax liability, proceed to step 2.

2. Administration Costs: Settling an estate can be expensive, especially the professionals that you need to hire. In addition, there are court costs associated with the Probate Estate. Also, if there is real estate, that too will be a source of expenses (mortgage payments, utilities, etc.). Your team and the court need to be paid or your efforts will stall. Mortgage payments need to be paid or foreclosure will ensue. Collect estimates of total fees from each team member. Ask your lawyer to estimate the likely court costs. Calculate real estate expenses for a

year. Add all of the estimated administration costs, the total projected taxes, and the real estate expenses. If the resulting figure exceeds the available cash, begin considering what estate assets you can sell. If your cash is still the larger number, then proceed to step 3.

3. Medical Bills: If your decedent was hospitalized or in a nursing home or assisted-living facility, there are going to be final medical bills, and lots of them. The billing practices of both physicians and hospitals can be woefully inefficient, with some bills arriving as late as a year after the date of death. And those that arrive sooner have often not been adjusted for health insurance payments. Therefore, don't even consider using the proceeds for matters discussed in steps 4 and 5 until at least a year has gone by. If, after paying taxes, administration costs, and final medical bills, you project that you will still have cash on hand, proceed to step 4.

4. Mortgage Payoff: Here is something I bet you didn't know: Death is considered defaulting on your mortgage. That is to say

that your mortgage company can foreclose on the house the instant you have breathed your last. They rarely do, of course. So long as they continue to receive mortgage payments—from anybody at all—they are happy. If you plan to sell the property, the mortgage will be paid off with the sale proceeds. If you plan to distribute the property to a beneficiary, the beneficiary will need to seek their own financing to replace the existing mortgage. However, if your beneficiary cannot replace the mortgage, you must pay the mortgage balance before you distribute the property. If that is the case, and you still have cash left over, proceed to step 5.

5. Beneficiary Buyouts: There is always at least one beneficiary who can't wait to get their share. The nagging, whining, and complaining, along with the threats and ultimatums, usually surface a few weeks after the death but have been known to commence as early as the funeral. In one instance, the youngest of three children called the executor, the court, and me every day for the entire duration of the probate process, which was three

years. Sometimes, you just want them to go away. And with sufficient cash to satisfy their share, you can do just that. However, you will first need to get the agreement of the other beneficiaries in writing.

Taxes

One of the great advantages of life insurance is that it is not subject to income tax. You will not be receiving a Form 1099 and, more importantly, neither will the IRS. If you doubt me, have a look at your 1040 and you will see that there is no line for it, nor is it mentioned anywhere in the IRS instructions. You get to keep all of it. And yet, it can be used to pay deductible expenses such as mortgage interest. From an income tax point of view, it is the perfect asset.

On the other hand, life insurance may be subject to the Federal Estate Tax. And it's not hard to find a line for it on the Federal Estate Tax Return; the IRS has dedicated an entire schedule to life insurance (Schedule D). The rule is that if the decedent owned the policy, then the death benefit (i.e., the insurance amount before the interest additions) is subject to the Estate Tax and most likely to your state's death tax(es) as well. However, if the policy is owned by anyone else, the proceeds are exempt from the Federal Estate Tax.

This little quirk in the law gave rise to the Irrevocable Life Insurance Trust (aka ILIT) some 60 years ago. In an ILIT arrangement, a trustee other than the insured is both the owner and the beneficiary of the insurance policy. When the insured dies, the trustee then files the claim for the insurance proceeds and distributes them according to the terms of the trust. Most often, the trust specifies the exact same beneficiaries that your decedent would have named as the life insurance beneficiaries. However, the insured doesn't own the policy; the trustee does. As a result, the exact same result is achieved but without incurring death taxes.

Of course, an ILIT is totally unnecessary if the life insurance is not pushing the Taxable Estate over the exemption limit (currently $5,450,000). So, for example, if a decedent had $3,000,000 in assets plus a $500,000 life insurance policy, an ILIT would be a wasted effort. On the other hand, if the decedent had assets worth $5,450,000 plus a $500,000 insurance policy, an ILIT would save up to $200,000.

Finally, the interest that is tacked on to the death benefit is taxed as income. It is not subject to the Federal Estate Tax.

Summing Up

Life insurance provides you, the executor, with much-needed liquidity. Most often, it takes the form of Term, Whole Life, and Accidental life insurance policies. Payments can be in a lump sum, installments, or even an insurance company checking account. And, although it is often difficult to claim, employing the assistance of your insurance agent greatly simplifies the process. The proceeds are most often used to pay taxes, administration expenses, medical bills, and mortgages. They can even be used to buy off an annoying, impatient beneficiary. Just be mindful of the major exclusions: suicide within two years, murder, fraud, and failure to pay the premiums. If an exclusion applies, there may be no insurance proceeds coming your way at all.

Things to Do

1. Contact the decedent's insurance agent and request the claim forms.
2. Provide your lawyer with the forms and the information necessary to complete them

(e.g., policy information, beneficiary information, mode of payment).

3. Follow up to be certain that the claim has been filed.

4. If the proceeds are payable to the Probate Estate or Trust Estate, be sure to provide your accountant with both the taxable and non-taxable portions of those proceeds.

Chapter 13
What's in It for You

The settlement of the vast majority of estates (all four of them) takes most people at least a year and manages to siphon off countless hours of your life in the process. The problems, the deadlines, and the stress are often palpable. As a result, the Law of Estates and Trusts has long recognized your right to compensation. And, as we shall see in this chapter, there are a number of ways your pay can be calculated and a number of ways for you to take it.

That being said, when it comes to what you get for your efforts, there are two schools of thought: yours and the beneficiaries'. It has been my experience that, to a beneficiary, all of your hard work does not appear to be all that hard. It is not unlike the old complaint that estate lawyers hear all the time: "Why do you charge so much for a will and a trust? All you have to do is push a button on your computer and out it comes." What can I say? For some, ignorance is its own reward. Do not let that dissuade you. You have accepted a job that holds you to the highest standard of care known to the law. You have accepted a job that puts you at risk of lawsuits, fines, and even jail time. And, not to put too fine a point on it, you have accepted the job that nobody else wanted. You deserve to be paid.

Reimbursements

First things first. You need to understand the difference between compensation and reimbursement. You are compensated for your time, but you are reimbursed for your out-of-pocket expenses. For example, being the responsible one in the family, it is not uncommon for the executor to put the funeral on his American Express card. Many times, after a respectable mourning period, the executor may bring this up, asking siblings or other beneficiaries if they couldn't see their way to "chip in" and reimburse him for some of the cost. The usual response is crickets. Not to worry. The estate itself owes you reimbursement and, once you have control of the Probate Estate or the Trust Estate, feel free to write yourself a check. You are well, well within your rights to do so.

And it is not just funeral costs that need to be reimbursed. You may not be from the same state as the decedent. You may, in fact, live thousands of miles away. But you have a job to do and that job usually involves being where the decedent lived. You are going to have to appear in the local court at least once to be made executor. You are going to have to survey the home, arrange for repairs, and get it ready for sale. It may be necessary to meet with family or other beneficiaries to calm their fears and answer their questions as a group (assuming e-mail is not a viable alternative). In short, unless you lived near the decedent, you're going to be traveling. And travel costs are reimbursed to you as well.

The cost of car, bus, train, or air travel are reimbursed using different standards. Car travel is reimbursed at 56 cents per mile (as of 2015). Bus and train fare are reimbursed at cost. Air travel, on the other hand, raises a question. Can you be reimbursed for a first-class seat? Since first class on most airlines can run from $1,000 to $5,000, it would seem to be an extravagance that the estate should not have to bear.

On the other hand, if you are living in California and your decedent was from Virginia, the cost of driving from coast to coast, and back again, including hotels and meals, is going to add up to at least $4,000. So, in reality, flying first class is less of an expense. Besides, when you agreed to take on this project, you did not agree to be a martyr—and nothing says "martyr" like riding 3,000 miles in coach.

In addition to funeral reimbursement and travel costs, you should take reimbursement for just about anything that can be considered an ordinary and necessary expense of settling an estate including, but not limited to, legal fees, accounting fees, court costs, home repair costs, bonding premiums, and so on. Ideally, you will pay for these things out of the estate's or trust's checking accounts but, if circumstances require that you pull out your MasterCard, be sure to write yourself a check.

It is important to understand that, although they often provide guidelines on compensation, Probate Courts rarely tell you what can be reimbursed. For our purposes, you are going to rely on the most conservative of all financial institutions—the Internal Revenue Service. Everything I have said about reimbursement comes from IRS regulations and guidelines. Most courts have absolutely no problem with that. And, bonus, it gives you grounds to dismiss the beneficiary who believes that your cross-country travel should be by pack animal.

Commissions

You have devoted a year or more of your life to settling your decedent's estate. Time to get paid. But how do you calculate your pay? There are four methods for calculating your commission: Stated, Formula, Court Decree, or Beneficiaries Agreement.

The Stated method of calculating your commission is a prime example of look before you leap. That's because many wills and trusts state what the executor or trustee's commission shall be. If the will or trust says that you get $10,000 to settle the Probate Estate or the Trust Estate, that's your commission. Except for out-of-pocket reimbursements, that's all you get. To make matters worse, some wills and trusts specify that the executor and trustee get nothing. The lesson to take away from this is to always read the documents that you are about to administer. Just because you are named the executor, doesn't mean you have to take the job.

The Formula method is the most common. Put simply, your pay is tied to the value of the estate you administer. For example, here is a common formula for an executor's commission:

First $400,000 of Estate Assets 5%
Next $300,000 of Estate Assets 4%
Next $300,000 of Estate Assets 3%
Estate Assets in excess of $1,000,000 . . . . .2%
Estate Assets in excess
   of $10,000,000 . . . . By agreement
                                   with the Probate Court

plus 5% of income generated by the Probate Estate each year.

Easy, right? So, for example, your estate had assets worth $800,000. In addition, the estate generated $10,000 in income (e.g., interest and dividends) during the year it took for you to settle it. According to the formula above, your commission is $35,500: $400,000 × 5% plus $300,000 × 4% plus $100,000 × 3% plus $10,000 × 5%. On the one hand, $35,500 is less than the average wage for a full-time job. On the other hand, settling an estate is not really a full-time job.

As noted in the formula, commissions on exceedingly large estates often require prior agreement by the

Probate Court. There is a good reason for this. Let's say, for example, that your decedent had only one asset. He owned $50 million worth of stock in a single company all held with one brokerage. It would be very hard to justify a commission in excess of $1 million to liquidate one stock.

On the other hand, perhaps in the course of your administration, the board of directors were suspected of insider trading. So you initiated a stockholder suit that dragged out for years, consumed your days and nights, took a toll on your health, led to your divorce but, ultimately, resulted in $100,000,000 in compensatory and punitive damages. The court may agree that you are entitled to your $1 million commission. Every case is judged on its merits.

The final method of calculating your commission is by Beneficiaries Agreement. There are times when even the beneficiaries agree that you are not getting paid enough. So, for example, your decedent owned two homes. Both are in horrendous condition when you take control of them. First, you have to enlist a realtor to tell you what condition they need to be in before they can be sold for a reasonable price. Then you have to get estimates from competing contractors to learn what all the repairs are going to cost. Then you have to dutifully monitor the pace and workman-ship of your contractor. Then you have to submit to county inspection. And so on, and so on, and so on. As a result, you put more time into unloading these fixer-uppers than anybody thought would be neces-sary. The beneficiaries may agree to give you more of a commission than the formula mandates. It is rare for beneficiaries to be generous, or even considerate, but it happens. The Probate Court will always accept this method of calculating a commission so long as the agreement of the beneficiaries was unanimous and put in writing.

Commissions Reduction

While an executor is, on occasion, entitled to more than the calculation provides, the opposite is also true. An executor may actually be entitled to less. This occurs in two situations: (1) when the executor hires someone else to do his job, and (2) when there are multiple executors.

The courts have long maintained that you are enti-tled to hire a lawyer to handle court proceedings or an accountant to prepare tax returns. However, where your lawyer has become the executor or the accountant has to dig through all of the decedent's papers to find the raw numbers needed to prepare the return, the courts tend to balk. The rule of thumb is that you accept the responsibility of being executor and you do the legwork that any layman can do. If you are delegating to the professional work that does not require professional expertise then the professional's fees will be deducted from your commission.

This is not necessarily a bad thing. If you are already too busy to complete even simple tasks, you have the right to delegate that work to others. So, if you don't really need the commission, delegation may be an ideal solution. Additionally, if the professional fees exceed what would have been your commission, you are not billed for the overage; the fees remain a cost of administration to be borne by the estate.

The second scenario requiring a reduction in your commission is where you have one or more co-executors. The rules generally require the commission to be divided evenly among the co-executors. A perfectly sound policy where the executors share the workload equally. It can become an issue, however, where the will names your broke, lazy, irresponsible, and occasionally felonious sibling to be your co-executor. The first thing you should do is ask your sibling to decline appointment as co-executor. The law does not force anyone named as executor to actually accept the responsibility. If that doesn't work, outline the tasks and responsibilities you expect your sibling to perform and then, for good measure, explain that neither of you gets paid until after the estate is settled. Use whatever other arguments you can conjure, valid or specious, to persuade the black sheep of the family that it just isn't worth it. Don't forget to mention the possibility of imprisonment. Trust me, you do not need to make your job any more difficult than it already is.

Tax Issues

Commissions

As they say, no good deed goes unpunished. You are entitled to compensation for your efforts as executor, but your reward is taxable. Well, at least it may be.

When a client comes in to do estate planning, I ask a lot of questions. One question is how they would like to compensate the executor and the trustee? I tell them that they have two choices. First they can say nothing in the will or the trust and leave it up to the executor and trustee to calculate the commission using a formula. Or, I tell them that they can make a bequest. The commission is taxable, the bequest is not. Now before you accountants out there jump all over this proposal with cries of "form over substance," allow me to explain.

The IRS does indeed live and breathe by the policy that if it walks like a duck and it talks like a duck, it's probably a duck. In other words, a taxpayer cannot extoll form over substance. Accordingly, the argument goes, whatever label we apply to it, something that is meant as compensation must be treated as compensation and, therefore, taxed. However, a bequest of say an additional 5% of the Probate Estate, 5% of the Trust Estate, 5% of the sum of the two or, for simplicity sake, 5% of the sum of all the estates, with no strings attached, is just what it appears to be, a bequest.

For example, in my father's trust, his five children were left equal shares of the Trust Estate. My younger brother, however, was bequeathed an additional 5%. And that was all I drafted the clause to say. He was not required to do anything additional for his inheritance bump. As a bequest, it was tax-free to him. Had I not been able to perform my duties as the trustee, he was next in line for the job. Unless he took a commission, he would not have been taxed in any way. Nor could the Internal Revenue Service argue that his additional 5% was actually a commission in disguise unless they wanted to argue that merely helping out turns a tax-free bequest into compensation—an argument I seriously doubt would prevail in court.

But, as they also say, nothing is perfect. If you bequeath an additional sum to the person you expect to settle your estate, you have to be certain that the person does not also take a commission. You could simply state that your fiduciary, whoever that may be, is not to receive a commission. But, in that case, should your intended fiduciary not settle your estate, for whatever reason, there is not a lot of incentive for anyone else to do it either. The best approach is to bequeath an extra sum to the fiduciary-apparent and trust that this trustee or executor will be honorable.

It bears mention at this point that, if you are the appointed executor or trustee and also the sole beneficiary of the estate, it makes absolutely no sense for you to take a commission. Why convert any part of a tax-free inheritance into taxable compensation? You are getting it all in any case, tax-free. On the other hand, if you are not the sole beneficiary, and you have not been left a little something for your potential services as the fiduciary, then taking a commission gets you something extra, even after taxes.

Deductibility

Commissions are classified as an expense of administration. As such, the trust or estate may deduct them on the fiduciary income tax return. If the deductions exceed the income, the loss is passed through to the beneficiaries. So, if you are both executor and one of the beneficiaries, you will at least get your share of the estate's deduction, thereby attenuating your tax burden somewhat.

Summing Up

If you are going to undertake the thankless chore of settling an estate, you are entitled to compensation. Your compensation can be established by the will or trust, it can be calculated by an accepted court formula, it can be decreed by the Probate Court, or it can be agreed upon by all of the beneficiaries. In addition to your commission, remember to reimburse yourself for any ordinary and necessary expenses that you have paid on behalf of the estate. Do not assume that an expense is extravagant until you have calculated the cost of the alternatives. Finally, remember that your commission is taxable but your inheritance is not. Enough said.

Things to Do

1. Use a book or spreadsheet to track your out-of-pocket expenses.
2. Reimburse yourself for out-of-pocket expenses.
3. Calculate and take your commission.

Chapter 14

Common Conundrums

Under the very best of circumstances, settling a decedent's estates can be complex and time-consuming. However, there is a common assortment of fact patterns that can make your job even harder. Let's look at the ones most frequently encountered.

Lost Will

It may be that your decedent signed a will but it cannot be located. Even if you know the contents of the will, you have to proceed according to the rules of intestacy rather than what you know to have been the decedent's wishes.

For example, let us say that your decedent was the single father of three grown children. You know for a fact that he disinherited the youngest of them in his will. That will cannot be found. In the absence of the will, the law is going to leave the Probate Estate to all three children equally. To make matters worse, you know that the will named you as executor and waived the bonding requirement. Assuming the court permits you to probate the estate as administrator, you will have to pay the bonding fee out of your own pocket and bonds can cost hundreds of dollars per year and are required until the estate is settled and the probate assets are distributed.

The only solution available here is for the youngest to acknowledge that he was disinherited and sign a document known as a disclaimer. By signing a disclaimer, he is treated as having predeceased his father. Provided he has no children of his own, his share passes to his siblings and the desired result is achieved. If he has children of his own, a lot more disclaimers are going to have to be signed, enough so that the siblings are the only heirs he has left. As for your bonding fee, the court usually has the discretion to waive it but there is no guarantee.

Inconsistent Estates

It is fairly common for elderly parents to put all of their trust in one child—the child who is the caregiver and, more often than not, actually lives with the parent. At that child's behest, or simply in an attempt to avoid probate, the parent makes the child a joint owner of all of the bank and investment accounts. It doesn't matter that the parent's will leaves everything to all of the children equally. When the parent dies, all of the bank and investment accounts belong to the caregiver child. That is because the accounts are part of the Contract Estate and not the Probate Estate.

The only practical way for an equal division to be achieved is if the caregiver child is willing to share. Surprisingly, this happens more than you might think—either because of love for the siblings or simply out of a desire to do what is right. On the other hand, the only way to compel the child to share is by proving that the joint ownership was obtained fraudulently or through the abuse of the parent. In either case, it is going to be an uphill battle.

Jurisdiction Problems

The laws across America are pretty consistent when it comes to which court has jurisdiction to probate the will. By far and away, the majority rule is that it is the Probate Court for the city or county of residence. In other words, if the decedent was a resident of Difficult County when he died, that is the Probate Court that has jurisdiction.

However, what if your decedent had two homes? It is not uncommon for seniors to spend summers in one state and winters in another. In such cases, the city or county where they spent the majority of months has jurisdiction. But it is also common for seniors to live part of the year with one adult child and then part of the year with another child and then part of the year with yet another child—all on a rotating basis with no actual home of their own. In that case, you would have to seek jurisdiction in the county where the decedent had lived the most days out of the past 365. Even then, the court is rarely required to accept jurisdiction.

Bequests to Animals

Either because they read it in the paper, see it on the news, or just hear a story about a friend of a friend who left millions to a cat, most people have an unshakable belief that you can leave money to your pet. Can you? The answer is a very lawyerly, "Yes and No." Strictly speaking, pets are every bit as much property as the dining room table and chairs. In fact, they come under the Knick-Knack Estate as tangible personal property. And, unless it is not incredibly obvious to you already, rest assured that the law does not permit us to leave property to other property. Accordingly, if your decedent's will leaves $50,000 to Fido, you have a problem. That is the "No" part.

The "Yes" part of my answer refers to the use of trusts. While you cannot leave money directly to your pet, you can establish a trust for the care of that pet. If your decedent had done that, the bequest in the will might read something like this, "I leave $50,000 cash to the Snowball Care Trust." If your decedent did not establish a trust but did, in fact, attempt to leave money directly to the pet, you may be able to convince the court that a "constructive trust" has been created and that you are willing to act as trustee. If that attempt is unsuccessful, you may be able to convince the beneficiaries, by written Beneficiary's Agreement, that whoever volunteers to take the pet gets the money. If that solution proves unworkable, then the bequest will fail and the cash will pass to other beneficiaries named in the will.

Bequests to Minors

Although not pets, minor children share the pet's legal inability to give receipt for an inheritance. That is because, like pets, they have no legal right to own anything. But if your decedent's will leaves money to a minor child, the bequest doesn't simply fail and it must be carried out. There are several possible scenarios that may present themselves.

First, if the minor is the decedent's child, the will may name a guardian of the child's property or the will may actually establish a trust for the minor, regardless of whether the minor is the decedent's child. Either way, someone is named to hold the minor's inheritance until a more suitable age is attained.

In the absence of a guardian or trustee, your only alternative is to petition the court to appoint a fiduciary known as a guardian ad litem. The guardian ad litem stands in the place of the minor, not just to receive and manage the minor's inheritance, but to give receipt for it, thereby allowing the executor to complete the probate process.

Squatters

An executor or trustee frequently finds that the decedent's real estate is occupied by someone other than an owner. Usually, this is a relative, friend, or even a romantic companion. In some cases, you will find that the will or trust has bequeathed the real estate to the tenant. But if it does not, you may have no choice but to remove the occupant.

On the other hand, several possible solutions present themselves. First and foremost, the beneficiaries who will be taking title to the real estate may agree to rent the property to the occupant. If the occupant is one of those beneficiaries, the other beneficiaries may agree to give the occupant title to the property as part or all of the inheritance. Or, if the real estate is worth more than the occupant's share, the beneficiaries may allow the occupant to buy them out. The number of possible solutions are endless. The problems arise when the occupant feels entitled to live there, rent-free.

In my experience, whenever the occupant is insisting they be allowed to stay, it's usually because they have nowhere else to go—usually because they are living on little income or government assistance. If that is the case, and no other solutions present themselves, then you have a fiduciary obligation to remove them. How difficult that will be is going to depend on where you are; it is not going to be pleasant in any case.

Mistrust

As an executor or trustee, there is nothing more unpleasant than dealing with feuding siblings. In most cases, the problem begins with one sibling who has been nursing some perceived slight or insult for decades. No matter how responsible and impartial you endeavor to be, that sibling will assume that you are siding with the enemy, that you are not to be trusted, and on occasion, will actually seek your removal. In one case, a sister was convinced that her parents were worth approximately 100 times what they were actually worth and that the Executor was helping the siblings hide 99% of the money.

Sometimes, there simply is no solution for this problem. Wild eyed, angry, emotional people do not negotiate. They will do all that they can to make your already difficult job even more difficult. In such cases, if you are the Executor, you may have no choice but to petition the court to allow your resignation. If you are the Trustee, you may simply resign.

Conclusion

As I said in the Introduction, people will read this book for any number of reasons. If you are a professional and you are adding settling decedent's estates to the list of services you provide, I hope that I have given you some idea of the challenges that await you in a new profession. It is a strange calling in some ways, but a rewarding one to be sure.

But if you are the executor for a loved one's estate, your job is doubly difficult. Not only must you undertake one of the most technically difficult tasks ever to burden you, you must do it all while grieving for your loss. In May 2010, both of my parents died—11 days apart. Despite my years of training and experience, settling their estates was far and away the hardest thing I had ever done. But I got through it and so will you. As a law professor once said to me on the eve of final exams, "This too shall pass."

GLOSSARY

ACCOUNT–A report to the Probate Court listing all of the Probate Estate's receipts, disbursements to creditors, distributions to beneficiaries, gains, losses, and adjustments

ACCOUNTING–The act of providing an account

ADMINISTRATOR–A person appointed by the Probate Court to settle the Probate Estate when there is no will or where the will does not name an executor

ANCESTOR–Anyone from whom you can trace your lineal descent (e.g., parent, grandparent, great grandparent)

APPRAISED VALUE–The value of real estate or tangible personal property as determined by a trained individual who may—but need not be—licensed for that purpose

ASSESSMENT–The value of real estate as determined by local government for the purpose of calculating and collecting real estate tax

AUCTION–A sale of tangible personal property

BENEFICIARIES' AGREEMENT–A contract between and among beneficiaries whereby the composition and timing of distribution of each beneficiary's share is determined

BENEFICIARY–Anyone who is entitled to money, real estate, or tangible personal property by virtue of the terms of a will, contract, or living trust

BROKER–A professional who buys and sells securities for investors

BROKERAGE–A company that employees multiple brokers

BUREAUCRAT–A government employee tasked with providing services to citizens (i.e., public bureaucrat) or a customer service representative for a large company (i.e., private bureaucrat)

BUY-SELL AGREEMENT–A contract between a business owner and someone who seeks to buy the business upon the owner's death

CODICIL–An amendment to a will

COMMISSION–Compensation paid to an executor or trustee

CONTRACT ESTATE–Assets whose distribution is governed by a contract previously made between the person now deceased and a financial institution (e.g., life insurance, joint bank accounts, and retirement accounts)

DEATH CERTIFICATE–A state-issued, one-page document certifying the death of an individual and containing, among other things, information such as the decedent's name, date of birth, date of death, place of death, usual place of residence, and Social Security number

DESCENDANT–Anyone who can trace you as an ancestor

DNI (Distributable Net Income)–Income of a Probate Estate or a Trust Estate that yields an income tax deduction for either estate when distributed to a beneficiary

ESTATE–Property of every type that previously belonged to the decedent

EXECUTOR–Anyone named in a will and appointed by the Probate Court to settle the Probate Estate

EXECUTOR CERTIFICATE–A one-page document, issued by the Probate Court, certifying that the person named therein is the court-appointed executor

FACE AMOUNT–A cash sum payable to the beneficiary of a life insurance contract upon the death of the insured

FAIR MARKET VALUE–The price a willing buyer will pay a willing seller for any asset of the estate or trust in an arms-length transaction

FDIC (Federal Deposit Insurance Corporation)–An independent agency of the federal government charged with insuring bank customer deposits against loss

FEDERAL ESTATE TAX–A tax on a decedent's combined assets known as Federal Taxable Estate

FEDERAL IDENTIFICATION NUMBER–(aka Employer Identification Number, or EIN) A nine-digit number used to identify a Probate Estate or a Trust Estate

FIDUCIARY–Generic term for an executor, administrator, or trustee

FIDUCIARY DUTY–A fiduciary's obligation to exercise the care of a reasonable person in the management or settlement of a Probate Estate or a Trust Estate

FIDUCIARY INCOME TAX RETURN–The annual income tax return (both federal and state) of a Probate Estate or a Trust Estate

FORM 1099–An annual federal information form providing the details of assorted types of income that have been paid to the recipient (e.g., interest, dividends)

FUNDING–The process of transferring assets of every type to a living trust

HEIR–The person who is entitled to the decedent's Probate Estate when there is no will (aka heir-at-law)

HEIRLOOMS–A colloquial reference to those items of tangible personal property cherished by beneficiaries of the Probate Estate

INTANGIBLE PERSONAL PROPERTY–Paper assets that represents tangible value elsewhere (e.g., cash, stocks, bonds)

KNICK-KNACK ESTATE–The decedent's tangible personal property, which includes those items of monetary value, sentimental value, and no value

LIEN HOLDER–Anyone who has a legal claim on real estate or personal property as the result of an agreement (e.g., mortgage) or court proceeding (e.g., mechanic's lien)

LIVING TRUST–An arrangement between the individual who is establishing it and providing the assets (settlor) and the individual managing the trust assets (trustee) for the benefit of others (beneficiaries)

MINOR–A natural person who is not yet old enough to be considered an adult under the law; usually younger than 18 years of age

MINORS CLAUSE–A clause in a will or trust that restricts the use of a minor's inheritance until a specified age

NATURAL PERSON–A human being

PENSION–A stream of income provided to a retired person—and sometimes a spouse—by a former employer or a government

PLEDGED SECURITY–Real or personal property provided as collateral on a loan

PROBATE–A court proceeding whereby an executor is given access to a decedent's assets, which cannot be accessed in any other way

PROBATE ASSET–Any asset that the decedent owned in his or her name alone; not in trust, not in joint name, and not having a named beneficiary

PROBATE COURT–The court responsible for the appointment and oversight of executors and administrators

PROBATE ESTATE–All of the probate assets

QUALIFICATION–The court proceeding whereby an applicant provides all the information and documentation the court requires to appoint the applicant executor

RETIREMENT ACCOUNT–(aka Qualified Retirement Account) The product of federal statute as well as IRS and Department of Labor regulations, it is a trust account that accepts deductible contributions that grow tax-free until the owner withdrawals it or reaches the age of 70 ½ years (e.g., IRA, 401K, TSP)

SECURITIES–Stocks and bonds

SETTLOR–The person who establishes a trust

STATE BAR REFERRAL SERVICE–A lawyer referral service made available to the general public by the state's bar association

STATE ESTATE TAX–A state tax on the decedent's combined assets

STATE INHERITANCE TAX–A state tax imposed on the recipients of the decedent's combined assets

SURETY–A form of insurance whereby the beneficiaries of a Probate Estate are protected from theft of malfeasance by the executor or the administrator

TANGIBLE PERSONAL PROPERTY–Assets other than real estate that have or once had intrinsic value (e.g., jewelry, furniture, coins)

TITLE COMPANY–A company that ensures that a buyer is acquiring good title to real estate through title search, document review, and title insurance

TRANSFER TAXES–Taxes imposed on the transfer of wealth from the deceased to the living and include Estate Taxes and Inheritance Taxes

TRUST ASSET–Any asset owned in name of the Trust Estate

TRUSTEE–A person who manages the Trust Estate

TRUST ESTATE–All of a decedent's Trust Assets

UNLIMITED CHARITABLE DEDUCTION–A Federal Estate Tax deduction for any bequest to a qualified charity

UNLIMITED MARITAL DEDUCITON–A Federal Estate Tax deduction for any bequest to one's spouse

WILL–A legal document that directs the distribution of the Probate Estate, nominates an executor, and sets forth the executor's powers and privileges

INDEX

DAVID G. HOFFMAN

In 1977, David received his Bachelor of Arts degree from Saint Joseph's University in Philadelphia, Pennsylvania. In 1980, he received his Juris Doctor degree from The Catholic University Columbus School of Law in Washington, D.C. While attending law school, he received the American Jurisprudence Award for excellence in advanced estate planning. David began his solo practice in 1983 and then became the senior partner with Hoffman & Mathey, P.C. in 2013. He has taught law for the University of Maryland, George Washington University, Northern Virginia Community College, as well as numerous technical schools. He has also lectured extensively for county and city governments, community organizations, private groups, businesses, and corporations. David has published numerous articles on wills, trusts, estate planning, estate taxation, estate settlement, and business formation. He is licensed to practice law in Virginia, the District of Columbia, and before the United States Tax Court.